WITH SCOTT TO THE POLE

The *Terra Nova* Expedition 1910–1913

The Photographs of Herbert Ponting

BARNES & NOBLE BOOKS
NEW YORK

2004 Barnes & Noble Books, New York

Published by arrangement with Book Creation Ltd., London, and
Book Creation LLC, New York
Publishing Directors: Hal Robinson and John Kelly

Dates listed underneath the captions in the portfolio and gallery sections are a guide to when the photograph was taken. In some cases, where the precise day is not known, the month or year alone is provided.

Contributors and consultants:
H. J. P ("Douglas") Arnold, Dr Liz Cruwys, Professor Julian Dowdeswell, Sir Ranulph Fiennes, and Dr Beau Riffenburgh

Special thanks to Professor Julian Dowdeswell for all his help and advice in the preparation of this book.

Designer: Peter Laws
Managing Editor: Tamiko Rex
Copy Editors: Jonathan Dore and Janice Anderson

Photographs on pages:
2. The Matterhorn Berg and Mt. Erebus (Clissold on summit)
3. Herbert Ponting and telephoto apparatus
5. Mt. Erebus and ice reflection in foreground

Front cover: Western Party crossing the ice to the *Terra Nova*
Back cover: Scott's Polar Party at the South Pole
Jacket flap photograph (back): Herbert Ponting and telephoto apparatus
Spine photograph: Steward Hooper eating baked beans on a wooden box advertising Heinz

Printed and bound in Singapore

ISBN 0-76075-627-9

10 9 8 7 6 5 4 3 2 1

CONTENTS

FOREWORD

SIR RANULPH FIENNES

FOR CENTURIES, JOURNEYS INTO THE UNKNOWN by explorers, merchants, scientists such as Darwin on the *Beagle*, or hunters such as those on the polar whaling fleets, told terrifying tales and sketched imaginative drawings to depict what they had seen, often with a good deal of artistic license.

The Antarctic wanderings of Captain James Cook in the 1750s and James Clark Ross in the 1830s were described in magazines and books with lurid illustrations of huge curling waves and towering icebergs, ever-poised above the tiny but heroic ships of the venturers.

Some seventy years later, when Britain first sent Torpedo Lieutenant Captain Robert Falcon Scott and his ship *Discovery* south to Antarctica, the box camera had been invented and was as vital a part of any expedition as a pith helmet or an ice axe. That was in 1901—the 20th century—yet Antarctica was still unexplored. Nobody even knew if it was a continent or merely a mass of floating ice. In 1910, Scott's *Terra Nova* expedition was sent to penetrate this vast and hostile region, to devise the best method of travel there, and, with a band of top-rate scientists under his control, to gain knowledge in the cause of science. He chose the best scientists from all over the Commonwealth as well as the best professional photographer-cum-cinematographer, Herbert Ponting, whose reputation was already firmly established in London after an exciting life in remote lands about which he lectured with magic lantern slides.

This book confirms Ponting was one of the truly great photographers of the 20th century, especially considering the extremely demanding conditions under which he had to work in Antarctica. In the 1970s, I worked as a photographer and cinematographer in Antarctica and even then, with vastly improved cameras, lenses, films, and ancillary gear, I still found even the simplest photographic activity extremely demanding in the ultra-low temperatures.

In the 1970s, a character-assassinating biography of Scott and a nine-hour equally distorted television program based upon that book attacked the explorer and his achievements. His posthumous record was besmirched and, in 2002, I decided to set the record straight and reassert historical reality in place of the groundless myths successfully propagated by the book and the film. I am delighted that my resulting book *Captain Scott* is now followed by this brilliantly produced Royal Geographical Society and Scott Polar Research Institute publication, which shows the stark reality of the conditions faced by Scott and his men, the very first human beings to penetrate and learn about Antarctica.

Christmas Eve in the pack on the way south.

Scott, Shackleton, and Amundsen were all brilliant polar travelers. All of the men made serious errors, but all achieved major successes. Amundsen was the first to reach the Pole, towed there by dog power; Scott was the first to arrive by pure man power. The US scientific station at the South Pole is called the Scott Amundsen South Pole Station in recognition of two great but very different achievements.

The greatest of French polar explorers, Dr. Jean Charcot, wrote in *Le Matin* (and remember that Frenchmen are not, by nature, inclined to be Anglophiles): "Scott has conquered the Pole. The public, ill-informed, will say that he reached his goal only second: but those who know—Amundsen and Shackleton among them—will say that it was Scott who opened the road to the Pole and mapped out the route, shedding a reflecting glow upon his country." He added: "Scott did not turn aside from his scientific program ... It is quite another thing with Amundsen. He is not a scientist. He is bent only on setting up a record. If one wishes to pronounce the one greater than the other, the preference must go to him who surrounds his expedition result with the greatest number of discoveries and scientific observations."

One of Amundsen's great Pole team members, Helmer Hanssen, said: "It is no disparagement of Amundsen and the rest of us when I say that Scott's achievement far exceeded ours ... Just imagine what it meant for Scott and the others to drag their sleds themselves, with all their equipment and provisions to the Pole. We started with 52 dogs and came back with 11, and many of these wore themselves out on the journey. What shall we say of Scott and his comrades, who were their own dogs? Anyone with any experience will take off his hat to Scott's achievement. I do not believe men ever have shown such endurance at any time, nor do I believe there ever will be men to equal it."

This book is a fitting tribute not only to Herbert Ponting, an artist of the highest quality, but also to a story of great heroism and courage.

Sir Ranulph Fiennes

CHAPTER ONE

THE ROAD TO THE POLE

BEAU RIFFENBURGH AND LIZ CRUWYS

The Road to the Pole

Beau Riffenburgh and Liz Cruwys

A century ago the Antarctic remained shrouded in mystery. It was seen as the last of nature's great secrets, the final blank, white space on the map. No one knew what the perpetual ice, the frigid temperatures, and the gale-force winds protected in the interior of this vast land mass that was larger than Europe or Australia. Was it covered by a giant icecap like that in Greenland? Was there simply an endless array of jagged peaks as in Norway's Svalbard within the Arctic Circle? Or did it consist primarily of an immense, low-lying barrier of ice that joined countless islands in a vast archipelago?

In the 1810s and 1820s commercial expeditions hunting for seals had explored much of the sub-Antarctic, concentrating on the region surrounding the South Shetland Islands, the tip of the Antarctic Peninsula, and the Weddell Sea. Then, during the following two decades, three major national expeditions—one British, one French, and one American—investigated and charted widely separated sections of coastline, helping to define the boundaries of what they thought might be a southern continent.

Of the three, the most successful was the British expedition from 1839 to 1843, which was under the command of Sir James Clark Ross. Sailing in HMS *Erebus* and *Terror*, Ross circumnavigated the continent and, south of New Zealand, became the first to force a way through the pack ice into the huge sea that now bears his name. Ross charted roughly 485 nautical miles (900 km) of new coastline in what he named Victoria Land before sighting an island on which stood two volcanoes that he named for his ships. (The nautical mile, equal to one-sixtieth of a degree of latitude or 1.852 km, was used by the naval explorers of Antarctica and is the mile unit used throughout this book.) Ross then discovered one of the Earth's most amazing geographical features, the vast expanse of ice—larger than Spain—that came to be known as the Great Ice Barrier and that today is named the Ross Ice Shelf.

Ross also managed to establish a new record for the farthest south yet reached, 78° 10' S, surpassing the 74° 15' S achieved by James Weddell some 20 years earlier. Strangely, despite these accomplishments, serious exploration of the Antarctic ground to a halt following Ross's expedition. For the next half century, the Antarctic slipped out of the public consciousness, and explorers, geographical societies, and governments turned their attention to opening up the great blank spaces on the maps of central Africa and the Arctic.

The return of Antarctic exploration to the international geographical agenda was, to a great extent, due to the long, lonely efforts of two men: the German scientist Georg von Neumayer and the British geographer Clements Markham. During the 1880s, each had independently, and unsuccessfully, argued for the benefits that could accrue if expeditions were sent to the far south of the globe. Then in 1893 Markham's power base grew considerably stronger when he became president of the Royal Geographical Society (RGS) in England. He immediately launched a new campaign for the revival of British Antarctic exploration, enlisting the aid of John Murray, Britain's foremost academic authority on the polar regions, in the matter.

Southern Cross *in the pack ice. Having first encountered the pack far north of where they expected it to be on December 30, 1898, the men of Borchgrevink's expedition were not finally through it until mid-February 1899. It then took them 12 days to unload all the materials required for the first wintering ever on the Antarctic continent.*

Murray and Markham made impassioned pleas for British scientific societies to back an expedition to the Antarctic to answer questions of meteorology, geology, and terrestrial magnetism, as well as to add to basic geographical knowledge. They also stressed that the research then being carried out on two Antarctic whaling expeditions was demonstrating the value Antarctic science might have on human understanding of the natural world.

Their persistent efforts to galvanize interest in Antarctic exploration were met with overwhelming support in 1895 at the Sixth International Geographical Congress in London. A resolution was passed stating that "the exploration of the Antarctic Regions is the greatest piece of geographical exploration still to be undertaken. That, in view of the additions to knowledge in almost every branch of science which would result from such a scientific exploration, the Congress recommends that the scientific societies throughout the world should urge, in whatever way seems to them most effective, that this work should be undertaken before the close of the century."

The Congress also advocated extensive cooperation between Markham's proposed British expedition and Neumayer's German one. The two men soon divided the Antarctic into four quadrants, assigning two to the British and two to the Germans. Both then began afresh their attempts to launch national expeditions to the region.

Before either was successful in obtaining official backing, however, they were beaten off the mark by a Belgian expedition under the command of Adrien de Gerlache. This sailed in August 1897 in the ship *Belgica*, with an international crew that included a Norwegian mate (Roald Amundsen), an American surgeon (Frederick A. Cook), and a Polish geologist (Henryk Arçtowski). All three men were to make indelible marks in the world of polar exploration and science. After visiting Tierra del Fuego and the South Shetland Islands, de Gerlache took his ship along the eastern side of the Antarctic Peninsula, where they discovered and mapped new islands and waterways before being beset in the ice. Unable to escape and confined to their ship, they became the first people ever to winter south of the Antarctic Circle, before finally breaking free in 1899 after 13 months locked in the ice.

Meanwhile another expedition was also underway—and it was one that was particularly galling to Markham, who was having difficulty raising funds for his expedition. This new expedition was led by Carsten Borchgrevink, an Anglo-Norwegian who several years earlier had claimed to be the first person to set foot on the Antarctic continent. Then, Borchgrevink had been a member of an expedition sent to determine whether there were enough whales in the Southern Ocean to support an Antarctic whaling industry. When a party landed at Cape Adare in Victoria Land (the coast that Ross had charted), Borchgrevink jumped out of the boat first. Although his claim to priority was inaccurate—the American sealer John Davis had landed on the Antarctic Peninsula as early as 1821—for the moment it gave him a certain amount of celebrity. Upon his return to Britain, he used this in an attempt to raise money for an expedition of his own.

After a couple of years of unproductive petitioning, Borchgrevink suddenly received from one source all of the funding he needed. The press baron George Newnes contributed £40,000, allowing Borchgrevink to purchase and outfit a ship that he renamed *Southern Cross*. With a crew primarily consisting of Norwegians—even though the expedition was officially British—they sailed south in August 1898. They landed at Cape Adare, where two prefabricated huts were assembled and a party of 10 was left to winter. This was the first scientific party ever to do so on the Antarctic continent itself.

During the next year, despite having inadvertently chosen one of the most exposed and harshest parts of the Antarctic coast, the party obtained extensive scientific data. However, their winter consisted of near misses with disaster and bitter feuds between Borchgrevink, who was far from a natural leader, and his scientific staff. When the spring came, the party was picked up and the men continued their investigation of the Ross Sea region. They found that the Great Ice Barrier had receded some 30 miles (56 km) since Ross's expedition, and on February 16, 1899, near what would become known as the Bay of Whales, the entire party disembarked to have their photograph taken at the farthest south ever reached by a ship. The next day Borchgrevink and two companions sledged over a featureless landscape for approximately 10 miles (18 km), reaching a new farthest south of 78° 50'.

Despite his record and the completion of a detailed scientific program, Borchgrevink's expedition was to a great extent ignored. His lack of leadership skills and his too-obvious efforts at personal aggrandizement overshadowed the expedition's accomplishments, as did his faulty handling of many of the scientific materials and records kept by his colleagues. Even more important, however, he returned to Britain at a time when attention was being given instead to the preparations for another expedition. Clements Markham was finally nearing his goal.

The flag at Cape Adare with the two Lapps who accompanied Carsten Borchgrevink's expedition, easily identifiable by their distinctive head gear. Borchgrevink named the base Camp Ridley in honor of his mother. He did not know that he had selected a particularly inhospitable part of the coast for his wintering.

Scott's British National Antarctic Expedition, 1901–04

In March 1899, the prospects for Markham's expedition had dramatically changed when Llewellyn Longstaff, a successful businessman and long-term fellow of the RGS, offered £25,000 to launch the project. Quickly thereafter the RGS and the Royal Society, which had joined forces in the venture, began developing plans for a purpose-built ship for the expedition. During the summer the government offered to donate £45,000 to the expedition on the condition that this sum should be matched by private subscriptions. With such backing, the additional monies were not long in coming—the British National Antarctic Expedition had been born.

Securing the finances for the expedition did not end all problems, however. The ensuing months would prove that the goals and plans of the RGS and the Royal Society were decidedly different. The representatives of the RGS held the view that geographical discovery was the primary objective of the expedition, while those from the Royal Society—Britain's most prestigious scientific organization—felt its purpose was to engage in scientific research. This ultimately led to a dispute over who should lead the expedition. The Royal Society wished to have the noted scientist John W. Gregory in charge, thereby following the same pattern of leadership as three other Antarctic projects that were then in preparation: the German expedition under Erich von Drygalski, a Swedish effort under Otto Nordenskjöld, and the Scottish research expedition under William Speirs Bruce.

Markham, however, had other ideas. He wanted the entire operation to emphasize geographical exploration rather than science and to be conducted under the auspices of the Royal Navy, in which he had spent his formative years. His choice as commander was the torpedo lieutenant of HMS *Majestic*, Robert Falcon Scott. Scott had first come to Markham's attention in 1887, when, as a midshipman, he had won a sailing race that Markham had been watching. Scott had neither the polar experience nor the scientific training of Gregory, but he was Markham's

On February 4, 1902, at what Scott named Balloon Bight, an observation balloon named "Eva" was filled and he became the first person to make an ascent in the Antarctic. He was followed by the third officer, Ernest Shackleton, and then by several others, although Edward Wilson, the junior surgeon, refused to go aloft; he described the efforts to do so as "perfect madness."

candidate, and Markham was an inveterate intriguer of championship caliber. With the help of another backroom powerbroker, Sir George Goldie, Markham ultimately forced his will upon the Royal Society, and Gregory resigned. With Gregory's departure the expedition became what Markham wanted: a voyage of geographical discovery in which science was subordinated to naval adventure.

Markham's influence went further than mere politicking for expedition leaders, however, and it would be felt in British exploration throughout the next decade. In the 1850s he had participated in one of the naval expeditions sent out in search of Sir John Franklin in the North American Arctic (Franklin and his two ships—coincidentally HMS *Erebus* and *Terror*—had disappeared in 1845), and this had shaped his beliefs regarding how a polar expedition should be conducted. Half a century later, he saw to it that the British National Antarctic Expedition was organized on much the same pattern, despite marked advances having been made in the interim, particularly in clothing, cooking, and travel equipment. Most importantly, he lacked any understanding of what had proved to be the most efficient techniques for polar travel: the use of dogs to pull sledges and the utilization of skis. He passed on to Scott his prejudice against these forms of transport and his bias in favor of the grueling task of man-hauling—using teams of men in harness to pull sledges—something at which the resolute and physically powerful Scott would prove to excel. However, the weaknesses in Markham's beliefs and practices would be shown all too clearly both on Scott's first expedition and then again a decade later.

The expedition finally left Britain in the purpose-built ship *Discovery* in August 1901. They reached Cape Adare, where Borchgrevink had wintered, in January 1902, before proceeding to the Great Ice Barrier. At the far eastern end they spied a peninsula that had never been seen before, which they named King Edward VII Land. They could not reach it due to heavy ice, however, and turned back toward the west. On February 3, they landed on the Barrier and the next morning an observation balloon was filled. Claiming the right to be "the first aeronaut to make an ascent in the Antarctic regions," Scott ascended some 550 feet (168 m). He was followed aloft by the third officer of

Discovery was tucked carefully into a small bay near the hut, where she spent the next two winters (right). The party actually wintered aboard ship, while using the hut primarily for work. The hut would prove to be a major staging point for later expeditions led by Shackleton and Scott.

Discovery, Ernest Shackleton, who rose to 650 feet (198 m) and took the first aerial photographs in the Antarctic.

The expedition now headed to McMurdo Sound, between Ross Island and Victoria Land, and at its far southern extremity they reached Cape Armitage, a peninsula where the island approached the Barrier. At a small bay nearby, Scott built his quarters, keeping the ship with them, rather than sending it north for the winter. As it turned out, the shelter that was built at what they named Hut Point was used primarily for work, while the members of the expedition lived aboard *Discovery*.

In the next several months, before the long, dark winter descended, the party fell into a routine of carrying out the necessities for living in a dangerous environment far from civilization, while at the same time conducting scientific observations. They also undertook sledge trips in order to become familiar with their surroundings. One of these—to Cape Crozier on the far side of the island—ended in disaster. When returning to base in a blinding snowstorm, a sailor named George Vince lost control on a slick surface and plunged over a cliff into the sea, never to be seen again.

Expedition members were taught the basics of skiing (above), which at that time included the use of one large pole, rather than two smaller ones. As the surgeon (and primary ski instructor) Reginald Koettlitz spent more time working on the downhill technique than on that of cross-country, his efforts were not as helpful as they might otherwise have been.

Once the winter was over, the program of geographical exploration began in earnest. Unlike the German, Swedish, and Scottish expeditions, the purposes of which were primarily scientific, Scott's main focus was a journey to the south. The goal was to cross the Great Ice Barrier, a move deep into the unknown, and there was wild speculation and hope that a three-man party might be able to reach the Pole, some 730 miles (1350 km) away. After an early reconnaissance and several depot-laying efforts, the main thrust began at the start of November. In mid-November, the support party, which had been man-hauling sledges with supplies for the polar party, turned back. Three men—Scott, Shackleton, and the expedition's junior surgeon, Edward Wilson—continued on their own.

Almost immediately problems arose. The three men had brought a team of dogs, but the opening weeks of the assault on the south had shown that none of them possessed the knowledge or skills to drive them efficiently. Now, without the aid of the support party, they found that the number of dogs they had were totally inadequate for the task of hauling all the equipment and supplies that had been left behind. The men were forced to join the dogs in harness and begin the onerous task of man-hauling. Even then, the sheer amount of material was too great to move, and Scott and his companions realized the only way forward was the back-breaking task of relaying. For the next month they moved south at a snail's pace, hauling their supplies three miles (5.6 km) forward and then returning for the second half, thereby advancing only one mile (1.8 km) for each three they traveled. It was not until mid-December, when they cached part of their load, including a great deal of dog food, that they were able to advance without relaying.

The highlight of the British National Antarctic Expedition was the southern journey that began on November 2, 1902. The three members of the main southern party, Shackleton, Scott, and Wilson, are photographed in front of their sledges and their individual sledging flags.

To their disappointment, even then the journey south remained maddeningly difficult, slowed by deep snow and the dogs doing progressively less work. They were also hindered by the fact that none of the three had a sufficient understanding of the use of skis, so that, although they had brought skis with them, they were carried on the sledge rather than used. This meant that the men frequently broke through the crust of snow that, on skis, they might otherwise have glided over. The difficulties of such arduous labor were compounded by their diet; it provided neither sufficient calories for the level of energy they were expending nor the proper nutritional balance. This was emphasized when, near Christmas, Wilson observed symptoms of scurvy (a vitamin-C deficiency that can be fatal if left untreated) in his companions.

Despite their precarious condition, the three men continued south until December 30, when they camped at nearly 82° 17' S. "If this compares poorly with our hopes and expectations on leaving the ship," Scott wrote, "it is a more favourable result than we anticipated when those hopes were first blighted by the failure of the dog team."

That dog team had also paid the price. By the time the party headed north on the last day of the year, only a handful of the original 19 were still alive. These were virtually useless, and the last pair were put down two weeks later by Wilson. In the meantime, the three men slowly dragged themselves and their sledges mile after mile on the seemingly endless journey across the unending plain of ice toward the north. On January 13, 1903, with their food running out, they spotted Depot B, where they had earlier cached their supplies. Their joy was somewhat offset by Wilson's diagnosis the same day that all three men were in the advanced stages of scurvy.

Shackleton, however, was more badly affected than the other two. He was frequently short of breath, coughed persistently throughout the night, and was by far the most fatigued. Soon thereafter this reached crisis stage, and Wilson forbade him to pull the sledge. He simply had to trudge along while his two colleagues did all the pulling. This continued for much of the next two weeks, and ultimately Shackleton donned the only pair of skis they had not discarded, which greatly eased his progress.

On February 3, 1903, nearing Hut Point after their long and arduous journey deep into the heart of the Great Ice Barrier, Scott, Shackleton, and Wilson were met by two of their comrades. The engineer Reginald Skelton and the physicist Louis Bernacchi pulled the sledge back to base with ease, where the three exhausted explorers were greeted as returning heroes.

Somehow, the weary travelers continued their trudge north. On January 28, they reached Depot A, a large supply of food and oil that had been set on the Barrier the previous spring. They feasted on delicacies they had not seen in months, and their worries about starving were at an end. But they were not home yet and, as if to prove the dominance of nature, that night the heaviest blizzard of the year swept down on them. In the thick, wet air Shackleton gasped desperately for breath and became so weak that he could hardly move. The three men stayed in their tent all the next day waiting for the gale to end, but rather than the enforced break proving beneficial to him, Shackleton became progressively weaker. That night, as the blizzard continued to roar outside and he lay helpless in his sleeping bag, Shackleton heard Wilson tell Scott that he did not expect the sick man to last the night. But that comment made Shackleton determined to pull through, and the next morning, although he was incredibly weak, he was ready to travel.

The three men now plodded forward past familiar landmarks, and on February 3, they were met by colleagues from Hut Point, who pulled the sledge back to base for them. Somehow they had reached safety.

In the ensuing days, while they recovered from their ordeal, Scott, Shackleton, and Wilson found out what had occurred in their absence. Beginning in November, the expedition's second-in-command, Albert Armitage, had led a party in an attempt to scale the mountains to the west of McMurdo Sound and find a passage up to the interior plateau. The result had been the discovery of the Ferrar Glacier, which, after many trials, Armitage and a number of his men ascended. In January they had finally become the first men to reach the vast polar icecap.

Late that same month, the relief ship *Morning* had arrived. However, *Discovery* was now separated from open water by miles of ice, and after a number of attempts to free her, Scott determined to stay there a second winter. *Morning* returned north with eight members of the expedition, including Shackleton, whom Scott deemed physically unfit to remain in the south, despite the younger man's protestations.

After a second winter, Scott again led a major sledging journey, this time following in Armitage's footsteps up the Ferrar Glacier. Once at the summit, Scott struck out onto the Polar Plateau for several weeks before returning to Hut Point in order to oversee the efforts to free *Discovery* from the ice. For more than a month and a half the expedition members labored to break loose. They were joined in early January 1904 by two relief ships, *Morning* and *Terra Nova*, which came equipped with explosives and an order from the Admiralty for Scott to abandon *Discovery* if they could not free her. However, on February 16, after weeks of constant work blasting a channel some 16 miles (30 km) to the open sea, a large explosive charge loosened the last ice trapping the ship, and *Discovery* was able to escape. After two and a half years, the expedition headed home.

Shackleton's British Antarctic Expedition, 1907–09

The next attempt on the Pole was made by Ernest Shackleton, who professed little interest in science and let it be known from the outset that his goal was explorative—to reach 90° South. To do this, he planned to employ two types of transport that had never been used in the Antarctic before: Manchurian ponies and a motor-car. Before Shackleton's expedition even sailed in 1907, however, he was confronted by a claim from Scott to have the sole right to use not only the *Discovery* hut, but all of McMurdo Sound. Scott wanted to lead another Antarctic expedition, and insisted that Shackleton should not go within hundreds of miles of their old base. This was an unreasonable

demand, particularly so considering that Scott had not at that time even discussed a second expedition with the Royal Navy. However, Shackleton considered Wilson a special friend, and since Wilson strongly backed Scott's position, Shackleton ultimately gave way. He promised Scott that he would make his landing at King Edward VII Land and not to go near McMurdo Sound.

But that was in London. When Shackleton's tiny ship *Nimrod* reached the Antarctic in January 1908, he found the situation not so cut and dried. The ship simply could not reach King Edward VII Land due to heavy ice, and a recent massive calving from the edge of the Barrier (a section breaking off and floating away) proved how disastrous it could be to set up a base there. So, loathe to break his promise, but feeling he had no choice, Shackleton led his men to McMurdo Sound. There the ice prevented them from reaching Hut Point, so Shackleton built a base instead at Cape Royds, 18 miles (33 km) up the coast of Ross Island.

The major problem with Cape Royds is that it is a small spit of land surrounded mostly by water and bounded on the east and southeast by the imposing slopes of Mount Erebus. These were too steep and too crevassed to allow safe passage to the south, so once the wind had blown the sea ice out of the Sound, Shackleton and his men were cut off from their goal until new ice formed. Prevented from laying depots for the Pole journey, Shackleton cast about for a task to keep his men occupied and their spirits high. The solution was obvious—they would make the first ascent of Mount Erebus (12,448 feet/3794 m). In early March 1908, five members of Shackleton's party overcame the technical difficulties of the mountain, their own inexperience and lack of equipment, and the frostbitten feet of their comrade Sir Philip Lee Brocklehurst to reach the top of the active volcano. Shackleton's party had made their first conquest.

At the close of winter, soon after the light had returned, but before the relative warmth had accompanied it, Shackleton began the process of moving supplies to Hut Point, the natural starting place for a southward journey.

In January 1904, Discovery*, still trapped in the ice, was joined by two relief ships,* Terra Nova *and* Morning*. Scott had been ordered to abandon* Discovery *if she could not be freed, but on February 16, a final explosive blast released her from the ice and allowed the expedition members to return home in their own ship.*

Shackleton brought with him an Arrol-Johnston motor-car (right), donated by William Beardmore, his initial sponsor and owner of the car-making company. Although the car played little significant role in the expedition, its presence marked a step forward in the use of modern technology in the Antarctic.

The first notable achievement of Shackleton's expedition was the ascent of Mount Erebus, which before Shackleton, had towered unconquered. In March 1908, a party of six departed from base (above) on what would become the first ascent of the snow-covered volcano.

Only three of the 15 members of the expedition had prior Antarctic sledging experience, and since it was too cold to use the ponies, circumstances forced Shackleton to introduce his men to the horrors of man-hauling. He had been obliged to readjust his plan during the winter, because he had originally calculated that he needed a minimum of six of the 15 ponies he had purchased to make the southern journey. However, only 10 ponies could fit aboard *Nimrod* and two of these had to be put down due to the battering they had taken on the voyage south. Four more had died at Cape Royds, a result of eating either the sand on which they were initially stabled or corrosive materials brought for the expedition. Shackleton had only four ponies, which meant he had to cut his southern party from six to four.

At the beginning of October, while Shackleton was laying a depot on the Barrier, three men left Cape Royds to fulfill the other major target of the expedition: reaching the South Magnetic Pole (which at that time was on land at about 71° S; constantly moving, it is now much further north, out to sea at about 65° S). This party consisted of the famed Australian geologist T. W. Edgeworth David; one of David's former students, Douglas Mawson, who would become one of the major figures in the Heroic Age of Antarctic exploration; and the Scottish surgeon Alistair Forbes Mackay. In a remarkable journey, the party man-hauled hundreds of miles up the coast of Victoria Land—relaying their loads much of the time—up onto the Polar Plateau, and thence to the Magnetic Pole, returning to the coast just in time to be picked up by *Nimrod*.

Meanwhile, the polar party—Shackleton, Jameson Adams, the surgeon Eric Marshall, and Frank Wild, who had been a seaman on *Discovery*—left Cape Royds on October 29. They soon discovered the disadvantages of using ponies rather than dogs in a glacial environment. The animals' hooves, carrying much more weight than dogs' paws, broke through the snow cover and threatened to plunge them down covered crevasses that dogs would have run lightly across. At the same time, they had to struggle constantly through snowdrifts up to their hocks and sometimes

In March 1908, a party of three was sent to climb Mount Erebus, with a support party of three more. Ultimately, the support party continued with the others, and five of the men—T. W. Edgeworth David, Douglas Mawson, Jameson Adams, Eric Marshall, and Alistair Mackay—completed the ascent, while Sir Philip Brocklehurst, who had frostbitten feet, waited for the others below the summit. Here four members of the party are seen at the crest of Mount Erebus's higher crater.

Shackleton was the first to experiment with ponies in the Antarctic. Here the four members of the southern party move ahead with their ponies each pulling a sledge. After Socks—the last of the four ponies—fell down a crevasse, the men were forced to man-haul the rest of the way.

their bellies. They also needed excessive care, having to be groomed, covered against the cold and wind, and fed large amounts of bulky fodder that had to be carried. The difficulties wore on the ponies, and one of them had to be put down a little more than three weeks after departure; this did have the advantage, however, of giving Shackleton and his companions fresh meat, which helped ward off scurvy.

By being able to pull heavier loads, the ponies did help Shackleton make much better time than when he had accompanied Scott six years before, and on November 26, the party passed Scott's farthest south, having reached that latitude in 29 days, as opposed to Scott's 59. But within a week, two more of the ponies began to fail and had to be killed, their meat either left at depots for the return journey or taken on with the men. The loss of the ponies meant that the men had to begin man-hauling, three of them pulling one sledge and Socks, the final pony, hauling another.

The Transantarctic Mountains, which had been visible to the west, now swung around in front of Shackleton's party, and in early December the men took the bold move of heading up a massive glacier that they hoped would take them through the mountains and up onto the Polar Plateau, while continuing to lead south. Soon, however, the move cost Socks his life; he plunged down a black, deep crevasse. Wild and the sledge only just escaped sharing his fate, when the harness attaching pony to sledge snapped before pulling them after him.

The four men spent the next three weeks slowly inching their way up "the Great Glacier," alternating between slick blue ice and snow-covered crevasses, at times making only a mile or two per day. By the time they exceeded an altitude of 10,000 feet (3048 m) on the Polar Plateau, they had been on partial rations for weeks, had been forced to abandon all their extra clothes because of the weight, and were becoming dehydrated from lack of oil to melt snow

Man-hauling was one of the hardest tasks ever assigned to free men (left). The heavy sledge and all its contents had to be pulled over high pressure ridges and across bottomless crevasses. Falls into the crevasses were not infrequent and the men were saved only by the harnesses attached between them and the sledges.

for water. They also faced temperatures as low as -25°F (-32°C) and strong winds blowing directly into their faces. But an indomitable spirit drove them on.

In early January, they realized that they would not be able to reach the Pole and return alive, so they made one final push to get within 100 miles (185 km). On January 9, they reached their farthest point south. "We have shot our bolt," Shackleton wrote that night, "and the tale is 88.23 S. 162 E." They had been only 97 miles (179 km) from the Pole.

The farthest south, at 88° 23' S on the Polar Plateau (above). Marshall took this photograph of (from the left) Adams, Wild, and Shackleton standing next to the Union Jack that Queen Alexandra had presented to Shackleton.

Now followed one of the most dramatic stories in the history of exploration, as Shackleton's party made a desperate dash north. Time and again they ran out of food and only just staggered to the next depot—across the Plateau, down the Great Glacier, and then over the Barrier. Each man collapsed at one point or another, to be helped on by his companions. As well as being a race for survival, it was also a race against time, as Shackleton had left orders that *Nimrod* could leave for New Zealand on March 1. But somehow they made it, Shackleton and Wild stumbling into Hut Point on the night of February 28, having left an ailing Marshall a day's march back in the care of Adams. They alerted *Nimrod* of their arrival, and the next day, despite his exhaustion from months of traveling, Shackleton led the party back to rescue Adams and Marshall.

Back in civilization, Shackleton's story instantly made him an international hero. He received a knighthood, and was honored and feted throughout the British Empire and the world. In all of this, the adoring public never seemed bothered that Shackleton, Wild, Adams, and Marshall had not actually reached the Pole. But there were a select few who were much more interested in what Shackleton had not accomplished than in what he had achieved. Among these was a man who had his own plans for the attainment of the South Pole—Robert Falcon Scott.

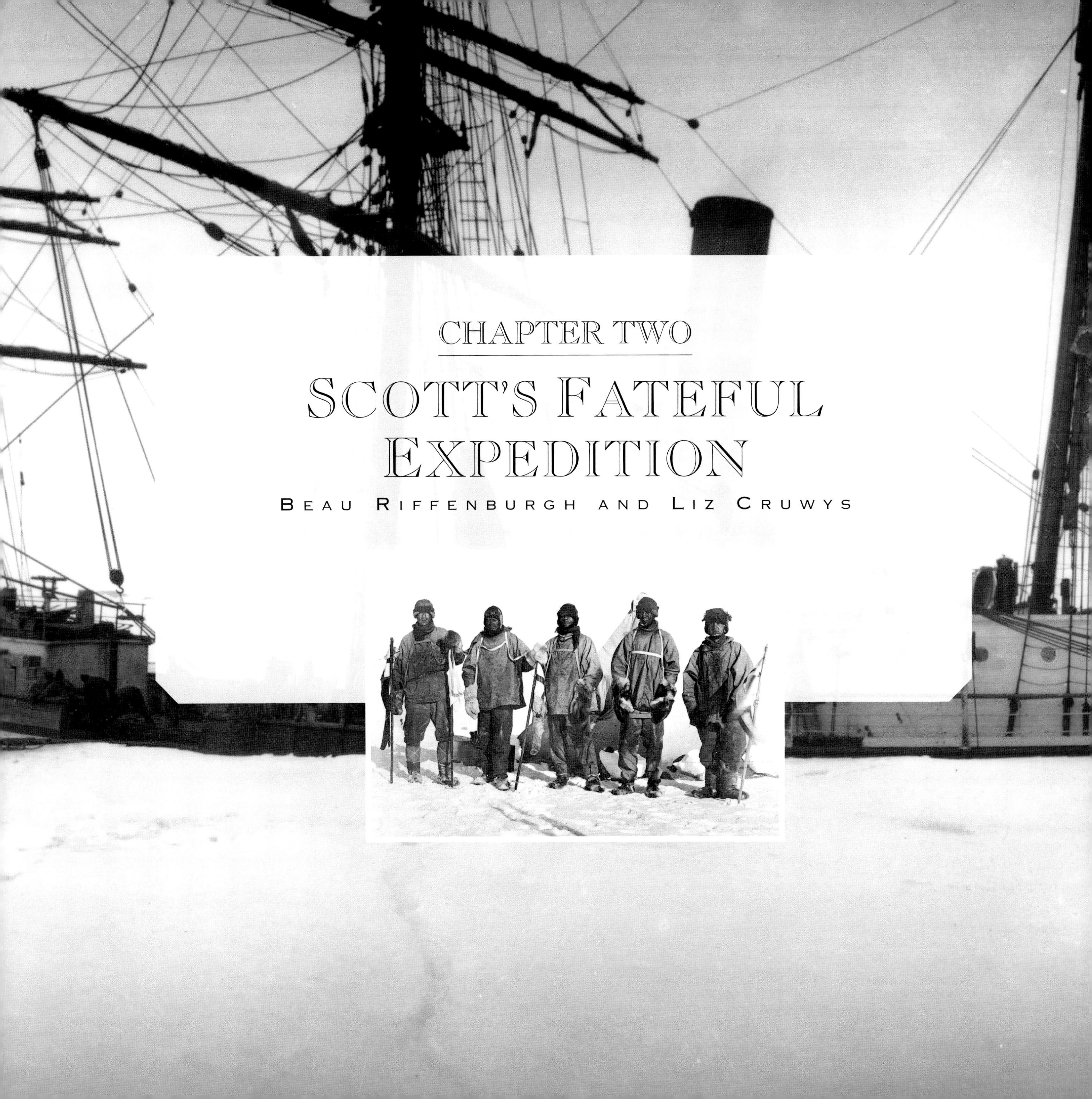

CHAPTER TWO

SCOTT'S FATEFUL EXPEDITION

BEAU RIFFENBURGH AND LIZ CRUWYS

SCOTT'S FATEFUL EXPEDITION

BEAU RIFFENBURGH AND LIZ CRUWYS

"A TRUE SPORTSMAN," ROBERT SCOTT SAID, raising his glass, "is not jealous of his record, or slow to praise those who surpass it." The scene was one of those that so bespeak the time that was Edwardian England. Filling the dining room of London's famed Savage Club were the glitterati of the geographical world, and sitting in the seat of honor was Ernest Shackleton.

But while Scott spoke no doubt very sincere words of praise for the achievements of his former subordinate, great must have been his inner joy at knowing that the South Pole was still surrounded by a patch of uncovered ground. In fact, while Shackleton had made speeches and presided over luncheons in New Zealand and Australia while slowly making his triumphant way back to Britain, Scott had continued with his careful planning for yet another assault on that most southerly of prizes.

So intense had Scott's early designs and strategy for another polar expedition become that, in the same week that Shackleton returned to London, Admiral Sir Lewis Beaumont, the vice-president of the Royal Geographical Society, had written a letter to the president, Major Leonard Darwin, indicating his view that the Society should stay out of any potential clash between the two explorers. The RGS, he stated, should encourage Scott to lead a scientific expedition without an emphasis on the Pole. "All of this long story is to incline you to put Scott off from making what I think will be a great mistake—that is, competing with Shackleton and organising an expedition to go over the old route merely to do that 97 miles."

Those 97 miles (179 km), however, were central to Scott's agenda, and on the evening of the very day that Admiral Beaumont wrote his letter, Scott provided a public glimpse of his intentions. In the after-dinner speech at the Savage Club, Scott turned from simply praising the commander and men of Shackleton's expedition, to urging that every future effort be made to assure that a Briton was the first to the South Pole. Indeed, he stated, he was willing "to go forth in search of that object" himself. "All I have to do now," he added, taking sardonic aim at the man he felt had betrayed him over McMurdo Sound, "is to thank Mr. Shackleton for so nobly showing the way."

Some three months later, on September 12, 1909, his intention was announced to the public, with Scott proclaiming that "the main object of the expedition is to reach the South Pole and to secure for the British Empire the honour of this achievement." For Scott himself, the aims of the expedition were not actually quite so simple. Although without formal scientific training, he had become very involved in the scientific studies carried out during his first expedition, and he was keen to ensure that a serious research program would add to the body of knowledge about the Antarctic on his next one. Yet he was not uninterested in the fame and potential fortune that could come from being the first man to reach the Pole. So, depending upon the audience to which he was speaking, he emphasized one or the other goal as the primary one, tailoring his message to attract the greatest possible public or scientific interest and funding.

The shore party (except Clissold, laid up, and Ponting, photographing) outside the hut at Cape Evans at the beginning of the fall, 1911. Standing from left: Taylor, Cherry-Garrard, Day, Nelson, Teddy Evans, Oates, Atkinson, Scott, Wright, Keohane, Gran, Lashly, Hooper, Forde, Anton, and Demetri. Sitting from left: Bowers, Meares, Debenham, Wilson, Simpson, Edgar Evans, and Crean.

During the following months, money was raised (including £20,000 from the government), the whaler *Terra Nova*—which had freed *Discovery* from the ice in 1904—was purchased and refurbished as the expedition ship, supplies and equipment were ordered, and Fridtjof Nansen was consulted. The famous Norwegian explorer who had been the first to cross the Greenland icecap and had later established a remarkable farthest north, Nansen had shown himself to be a genius at polar logistics, travel, and design of equipment. It had become one of the tasks of virtually every serious polar traveler to consult Nansen for his advice on a wide range of matters.

One of the most significant things that Nansen discussed with Scott was the proposed modes of transport toward the Pole. This was not an easy topic, because Scott had decided that several distinct methods would be used together. Nansen's recommendation was that the British expedition should follow the pattern of the most successful efforts in the Arctic and use skis in conjunction with dogs pulling sledges. Although Scott acquiesced regarding skis in the face of Nansen's arguments—and as the result of a demonstration of their efficiency when used by an expert—he was less than wholehearted about the use of dogs, undoubtedly recalling the problems he had encountered with them on his first expedition. He would take dogs, but it was only late in the expedition that he realized how well they could perform when expertly handled, and that he had brought too few to accomplish all the heavy pulling tasks they might have done.

Part of Scott's hope was placed on tracked motor sledges, which Commander Reginald Skelton, the former engineer of *Discovery*, had been helping to design, develop, and test for the previous two years. Despite the difficulties encountered on his first expedition, Scott also expected to man-haul. But the proposed method of transport that Nansen simply could not understand was the one that followed Shackleton's example of using Manchurian ponies. He argued strongly against them being taken. Nevertheless, ignoring the numerous difficulties with ponies that had been revealed all too clearly by his predecessor, Scott rather quixotically adopted them as a major part of his grand plan, going so far as to order only white ponies, because Shackleton's lighter ponies had lived longer than the darker ones.

Meanwhile, the naval officers and crew and scientific staff were also being selected. This was no easy task, as the expedition office received more than 8,000 applications. One of the first men invited to go had been Wilson, who was eventually named chief of the scientific staff, zoologist, and expedition artist. Part of his duty was to help Scott put together a large, well-equipped scientific team that would be able to carry out research at a variety of locations. A great help to them in this was T. W. Edgeworth David, the renowned professor of geology at the University of Sydney, who had led the party that had been first to reach the South Magnetic Pole on Shackleton's *Nimrod* expedition. One of the men Scott desperately wanted to join the expedition was David's former student Douglas Mawson, who had made major contributions to Shackleton's expedition. Although he decided to organize his own expedition instead, Scott's entire geological complement was eventually composed of David's former students or men who had worked under him: Griffith Taylor, Frank Debenham, and Raymond Priestley.

Oates with some of the 19 Manchurian ponies that were taken to the Antarctic for Scott's expedition.

The scientific staff also included two biologists: Edward Nelson, who would be part of the land party, and Dennis Lillie, who would remain aboard *Terra Nova* when she sailed back to New Zealand and then returned the following year to pick up those who wintered in the Antarctic. The meteorologist was Dr. George Simpson, on loan from the Indian Weather Bureau, and the physicist was the Canadian Charles Wright. As assistant zoologist, Scott was finally persuaded to accept Apsley Cherry-Garrard, the cousin of Reginald Smith, Scott's publisher and friend. Cherry, as he became known, had no scientific qualifications but was a protégé of Wilson, and this, together with the fact that he offered to pay £1,000 to join the expedition, persuaded Scott to take him.

Funding had also played an important role in the selection of two other members of the expedition. The first of these was the 28-year-old Royal Navy Lieutenant E. R. G. R. "Teddy" Evans, who had been second officer aboard *Morning* on the relief expeditions for *Discovery*. He had begun to organize an expedition of his own before being united with Scott by Markham, who recognized in the energetic Evans the ability to interest potential contributors and to raise more much-needed money. In return for being named second-in-command, Evans abandoned his own plans, added the funds he had already raised to those for Scott's expedition, and took over the supervision of the refurbishing, customizing, and stocking of *Terra Nova*. Unfortunately, their totally different temperaments meant that the two men would never be close, and there would exist between them only an uneasy alliance.

The other man whose involvement in the expedition was in part due to his money was a captain in the 6th Inniskilling Dragoons: Lawrence Edward Grace Oates, who soon came to be known as "Titus" by the other expedition members. An upper-class cavalry officer who had received a serious wound in the leg during the South African War, Oates offered £1,000 and his services for free should he be accepted. His love of and expertise with horses made him a natural to serve as the man in charge of the ponies.

Strangely, however, Oates's expertise was not used to its full advantage. He proved to be such a hard-working addition aboard *Terra Nova* during her preparations that Evans asked Scott if he could be kept aboard as a midshipman rather than being sent to Siberia to select the ponies. Scott agreed, but it was a critical error. Those who went instead were Cecil Meares—a superb dog-driver who had joined the expedition as the man in charge of the dogs—and, to help bring the animals from Vladivostok to New Zealand, Wilfred Bruce, Scott's brother-in-law. Despite his expertise with dogs, Meares knew little about horses. Thus, the ponies selected were, according to Oates when he saw them later, an exceptionally sad lot—too old, too diseased, too lame, and too full of a catalogue of other defects to be adequate for the work they would be expected to carry out.

Just as problems arose with the ponies before the expedition sailed for the Antarctic from New Zealand, the motor sledges also suffered an early setback. Once in place, Evans told Scott that he did not feel it appropriate that Skelton, who outranked him, should be serving under a junior officer. In response to Evans's concern, in March 1910, Scott released Skelton, who felt slighted after more or less being promised the position of second-in-command himself. Ultimately more significant was that Skelton was the only man on the expedition who really understood the motor sledges. His successor, Bernard Day—who had been in charge of Shackleton's motor-car on his 1907–09 expedition—never was as familiar, efficient, or productive with the motor sledges as Skelton.

Some six weeks before the expedition was due to sail, three other key officers joined the ship. Lieutenant Victor Campbell, who was to be the acting first mate, was a martinet with a short fuse and an explosive temper, but one who proved a remarkably efficient officer. Lieutenant Henry Bowers of the Royal Indian Marines, the officer in charge of supplies, had a seemingly infinite capacity for hard work and was a master of meticulous planning. And Lieutenant Harry Pennell was named navigator and was placed in charge of the ship's magnetic work. Considered by Wilson to be "by far the most capable man on the whole expedition," Pennell would ultimately take command of *Terra Nova* once the shore party had been left in the Antarctic.

The *Terra Nova* Sets Sail

On June 15, 1910, *Terra Nova* sailed from Cardiff, where she had put in for her last stop in Britain. This was a sign of appreciation both for the large contributions raised there for the expedition's coffers and for generous donations of coal, oil, and scientific equipment. The master of the ship was Evans, as Scott had decided to remain in England to continue raising funds. Two months later, when the barque that Wilson described as having two speeds—"slow and slower"—arrived at Simonstown, South Africa, they were met by Scott, who had arrived by (fast) steamer. The first two months under Evans had been a relatively lighthearted time in which the men had taken the opportunity to get to know each other. Now, with "the Owner" (as Scott was jocularly referred to) assuming command, the expedition took on a much more serious tone, as he began to assess those aboard in order to determine who would join the land party and who would remain with the ship.

As Terra Nova *entered the pack, the men aboard had no idea how long they were to be unexpectedly slowed down. Here, three members of the expedition survey the pancake ice stretching off into the distance.*

One early determination was that Campbell would lead the so-called Eastern Party. Scott's plan was for there to be, in essence, two shore parties. The major one, to winter in McMurdo Sound as close to Hut Point as possible, would include both the members of the Polar Party and the majority of the scientists, several of whom would go to nearby sites of special scientific interest, such as Dry Valley (now known as Taylor Valley). A smaller party, consisting of Campbell and five other men, was to be landed on King Edward VII Land, which had been seen by earlier expeditions but never actually reached. This meant that the members of the Eastern Party would be in an even

One of the most dangerous activities aboard a sailing ship was furling the sails in wild weather. In the midst of the ice pack, conditions might not have been as rough, but the men shown here furling Terra Nova's *mainsail would still have had to struggle with cold hands while far above the deck.*

better position to make new geographical discoveries than those with Scott. Who would belong to which party, or remain with the ship, was therefore a topic of great interest for everyone. But as the ship sailed slowly toward Australia, Scott, as later he would do throughout the expedition, kept his own counsel on personnel assignments, and announced them only in his own time.

On October 12, *Terra Nova* arrived at Melbourne, and suddenly Scott had other, alarming things to ponder. Waiting for him was a message that he read with puzzlement and then increasing irritation. "Beg leave to inform you," it stated, "*Fram* proceeding Antarctic. Amundsen."

What did it mean? No one was certain. It was common knowledge that Roald Amundsen, the Norwegian explorer who several years before had become the first man to navigate the Northwest Passage, had borrowed Nansen's ship *Fram* to make a polar drift in the Arctic basin. His goal had been to be the first man to the North Pole, and, although that possibility seemed to disappear when the Americans Frederick A. Cook and Robert E. Peary had independently claimed to have attained the Pole in September 1909, Amundsen had steadfastly stuck to his plan. Or so it had seemed. Now Scott questioned Tryggve Gran—the young Norwegian he had hired as a ski expert at Nansen's recommendation—but he knew no more than anyone else.

It would be more than two weeks—by which time Evans had taken *Terra Nova* to the harbor of Lyttelton, New Zealand, and Scott had reached that dominion's capital of Wellington after trying to raise funds on a trip across Australia—before they began to hear rumors of a challenge for the Pole. But they were just that: rumors. There was little hard evidence. Was Amundsen trying to beat Scott to the base in McMurdo Sound? Was he heading to the Weddell Sea on the far side of the continent? No one knew for sure. But at that point Amundsen's behavior, although an annoyance and a subject for a debate on the ethics of exploration, was not seen as a threat by most of the members of the British expedition. There was one man, however, who took a very different view, realizing that Amundsen was quite capable of snatching the Pole from the grasp of the British. "If he gets to the Pole first we shall come home with our tails between our legs and no mistake," Oates wrote in a letter to his mother. "They say Amundsen has been underhand in the way he has gone about it but I personally don't see it is underhand to keep your mouth shut—I myself think these Norskies are a very tough lot ... they are very good ski-runners while we can only walk, if Scott does anything silly such as underfeeding his ponies he will be beaten as sure as death."

Three days after Oates wrote those words, *Terra Nova* sailed for Port Chalmers, at the bottom of New Zealand's South Island, to take on a final supply of coal before heading for the Antarctic. There was hardly any room left aboard for it. During the weeks in Lyttelton, more had been forced into the holds and tied down on the decks than would have been believed possible when they left Britain. After Bowers had recounted and restowed the supplies already aboard, he oversaw the packing of tons of food and other materials donated by the generous New Zealanders. Then the three motor sledges in their huge crates were lifted aboard.

Shortly before departure, the 19 Manchurian ponies that had been held in quarantine on Quail Island in Lyttelton Harbour since their arrival from Russia were placed in stables that had been constructed on the ship's upper deck and under the fo'c'sle. Oates felt the amount of fodder that had been purchased for the animals was woefully inadequate, and managed to persuade Scott to increase it, before also cleverly loading an additional five tons he had paid for himself. Meanwhile, Meares constructed places on deck for his 33 Siberian sledge dogs, and then had to find quarters for himself, Bruce, and two Russians who had helped them transport all the animals from Vladivostok: the jockey Anton Omelchenko, who was to serve as a groom for the ponies, and Demetri Gerof, an experienced dog-driver who would help handle the dogs.

When Terra Nova *reached the pack ice on her way south, Ponting willingly took risks to make his record of the journey. Three planks were extended 10 feet (3 m) from the ship to form a small platform on which he could lie with his cinematograph, in order to film the ship's battles with the ice. He had to grasp the camera with one hand, and turn its handle with the other, hoping not to be thrown into the slush below.*

Also joining in New Zealand (and therefore packing the ship even tighter) were the Australia-based contingent—Taylor, Debenham, Priestley, and Day—as well as an itinerant photographer whom Scott had employed to make a careful record of the expedition. His name was Herbert Ponting but, although he was celebrated for the wonderful photographs he had taken throughout the world and had just that year published the fine photographic book *In Lotus-Land: Japan*, he preferred to be known, not simply as a photographer, but as the grander sounding "camera artist."

There were undoubtedly members of the expedition who initially had their doubts about Ponting, as he seemed fussy, prim, and demanding. As he later wrote in his book *The Great White South*: "Life on the *Terra Nova* was a very different matter to travelling on comfortable ocean liners"—the kind of observation that would have done little to endear him to men who had spent years at sea in difficult conditions. And to a crew working shifts and sleeping in hammocks located directly beneath the leaky planking where the ponies were stabled, it would have seemed strange that this fastidious man "found it almost impossible to sleep below deck in the narrow, stuffy cabins, crowded with our personal belongings." It would not be long, however, before the photographer Herbert Ponting won the respect of his shipmates, engaging in all manner of contortionist efforts to obtain the best possible photographs and footage with his cinematographic camera. He climbed the rigging in high winds; had a specially designed frame placed over the side of the ship so that he could film with his moving-picture camera from what proved to be a most precarious position; and he worked all times of day and night to record the members, events, and general images of the expedition. He quickly changed from an oddity to a highly valued colleague.

Terra Nova was just two days out of Port Chalmers when a gale of enormous proportions swept down on the heavily laden ship and almost ended the expedition before it even reached the Antarctic. Giant bags of coal and canisters of oil hurtled about the deck as huge waves broke clear over the top of the ship. The main pump failed, and all available men had to be set to bailing, a chain of hands passing buckets of water out of the boiler room, which was quickly filling with water, and up to the deck.

The ship was, in fact, slowly filling with water and sinking, and no amount of human bailing was going to keep it from disappearing into the depths of the ocean. The pump simply had to be repaired. But it proved impossible to open the hatch to the pump, so 12 agonizing hours were spent creating another path to its suction well. A hole was cut through the engine-room bulkhead, some of the coal in this next compartment was removed, and another hole was cut from there into the suction well. Teddy Evans then wriggled past the remaining coal, squeezed through the small hole, and found his way down the pump shaft. He cleared the suction mechanism of the coal balls that had formed from a mixture of coal and oil, and, free from this choking mixture, "to the joy of all a good stream of water came from the pump for the first time." The ship had been saved, although not without some cost. Two ponies, one dog, 10 tons of coal, and 65 gallons of petrol had been lost.

As the ship headed south, Scott began giving serious consideration to landing the main part of the expedition at Cape Crozier, at the eastern end of Ross Island, rather than in McMurdo Sound at its western end. This would allow them to land earlier, since they would not have to wait for the ice to clear out of the Sound; it would mean that the sea ice (or lack of it) would not affect the summer depot parties, as it had Shackleton's; it would give direct access to the Barrier at a point with fewer crevasses than the route south from McMurdo; and it would allow Wilson the opportunity to study the unknown behavior and incubation of the nearby Emperor penguins.

Before such considerations could be taken into account, however, *Terra Nova* faced another problem. On December 7, the first ice was sighted, and although this excited the men, it was considerably farther north than had been expected. Two days later the ship entered the pack ice that protected the northern reaches of the Ross Sea.

Terra Nova's *passage through the pack ice took much longer than Scott had anticipated. One of the few benefits of the time she was held captive in the ice was the chance it gave Ponting to take a wealth of marvelous photographs. This one clearly shows the difficulties an old wooden ship would have trying to force its way through heavy pack ice.*

Scott had expected to move through the pack rapidly, as it had taken only four days for *Discovery* to pass it and even less for *Nimrod*. But fortune did not smile on Scott this time. For 20 days *Terra Nova* remained mired in the midst of the ice, at times moving so slowly that Gran was able to begin training his comrades in the use of skis on nearby floes. It was only early in the morning of December 30 that the ship was finally free of the ice and plying its way south through the rough Antarctic waters. More than time had been lost—it had taken 61 tons of coal to break through the pack, and that would have an impact on how long the ship could remain in the south and how far she could transport various landing parties later.

Several days later another disappointment awaited. The heavy swell at Cape Crozier made disembarkation impossible, and Scott reluctantly ordered a turn to the west and McMurdo Sound. Perhaps the most disappointed of the party was Ponting, who had been promised the chance to photograph and film the Barrier. But the extra time spent in the ice meant that coal was too precious for such non-compulsory ventures. "With a heavy heart I then impotently watched the bastioned rampart slowly disappear astern," Ponting later wrote, adding, "one of the most remarkable features of the Earth, to see which, and in the hope of illustrating it … I had come over more than a third of the circumference of the globe."

The ponies and dogs were off-loaded before the supplies, because there were fears for their health after being cooped up for so long in small spaces without proper exercise. The ponies caused particular concern, and two had been so badly battered on the voyage south that they had to be destroyed. The dogs were passed over the side in a sling-like contraption, while the ponies were lowered in crates.

The Base at Cape Evans

They now made good time to McMurdo Sound, and on January 4, 1911, finding the way to Cape Armitage blocked by ice, Scott decided to establish his base at a small promontory that had been dubbed "the Skuary" during his previous expedition (since it was a nesting ground for large numbers of skuas), a dozen miles or so north of Hut Point. This he immediately renamed Cape Evans in honor of his second-in-command.

The work of unloading began immediately, the ponies and dogs being taken to shore that day, as well as two of the motor sledges and most of the prefabricated elements for the hut that would house them through the winter. For the next week the members of the expedition were very busy. While the hut was being built, the pulling power of ponies, dogs, and sledges was used to take the stores ashore.

On January 8, however, disaster struck. On this day it was decided to unload the third of the motor sledges and take it ashore. In the days that had passed since the other sledges had been unloaded, the ice had thawed and become progressively weaker, and the third sledge plunged through one such weak point—over which, only the day before, one of the other sledges had hauled a heavy load. None of the men hauling the motor sledge was injured but, according to Scott, "It's a big blow to know that one of the two best motors, on which so much time and trouble have been spent, now lies at the bottom of the sea."

The same week a second calamity on the sea ice was narrowly averted. Ponting, who was constantly recording the events of the moment, went onto an ice floe to photograph a pod of killer whales. Undoubtedly thinking him a seal, the killer whales bumped the bottom of the floe in order to knock him into the water—typical behavior for the giant predators. The floe broke and Ponting leapt to the next one, pursued by the voracious killers. As his comrades looked on helplessly, the camera artist managed to scramble with his camera from floe to floe just out of reach of the killer whale's hungry jaws. "What irony of fate to be eaten by a whale thinking one was a seal," Campbell wrote to his sister after Ponting's escape, "and then be spat out because one was only a photographer." Ponting would not have been pleased.

By January 18 the hut—a spacious 50 feet (15.2 m) long by 25 feet (7.6 m) wide—was ready to be occupied. It was divided into two major sections, with officers and "lower deck" segregated by a wall of packing cases. But the layout of the accommodation mattered little at that stage, because only a limited number of men would initially remain there. With no time to waste before the summer began to wane and the cold, dark winter drew on, Scott had no fewer than four parties setting out from Cape Evans.

Scott left first, with a group of 12 men, eight ponies, and two dog teams, making their way south to Hut Point and thence onto the Barrier to lay depots in preparation for the next spring's attempt on the Pole. The next departure shortly thereafter was the five-man Western Party led by Griffith Taylor and consisting of Debenham, Wright, Petty Officers Edgar Evans, and Robert Forde. This headed for the mountains on the western side of McMurdo Sound to make a geological examination of the region between Dry Valley and the Koettlitz Glacier. Meanwhile, a four-man party consisting of Ponting, Day, the biologist Nelson, and Chief Stoker Bill Lashly, was to go on a 10-day photographic trip to Cape Royds.

It might not look like much, but the hut at Cape Evans seemed like paradise to the members of the expedition whenever they ventured away from it, particularly on long sledging journeys. Today, the hut still stands strong and proud in its desolate location, but it is accompanied by an eerie feeling of tragedy, as if it still remembers what happened so long ago.

The final group was the six-man Eastern Party under Campbell, which consisted of the geologist Priestley, the surgeon Murray Levick, Petty Officers George Abbott and Frank Browning, and Able Seaman Harry Dickason. After dropping off Taylor and his colleagues, *Terra Nova* made for King Edward VII Land, where Campbell's small party was to be landed. The intention was that, following the erection of a hut, they would set out to discover as much as possible both geographically and scientifically about the region. But after proceeding along the Great Ice Barrier, they found that there would be no possibility at all of reaching their destination, which was surrounded by vast fields of sea ice interspersed with countless icebergs. They reluctantly turned back west, hoping to find some point where they could land on the Great Ice Barrier.

On February 3, *Terra Nova* sailed into the indentation in the Barrier that three years before Shackleton had named the Bay of Whales. Campbell had hoped it would make a good landing place, but to his horror he found it already occupied. There, nestling against the ice edge, was *Fram*. Amundsen had not only come to the Ross Sea, but was firmly ensconced in a camp three miles (5.6 km) inland, having arrived at the Barrier three weeks previously. The following day Amundsen visited *Terra Nova* and invited Campbell, Pennell, and Levick to breakfast at his base, which he had named Framheim. The British explorers were impressed by the magnificence of the Norwegians' temporary home, which included a sauna, a massive library, and a carefully designed setup for some 110 dogs. They were also well aware that Framheim's location placed Amundsen a full 60 miles (111 km)—one whole degree—closer to the Pole than was Scott based at Cape Evans.

In this photograph, Ponting has captured the natural beauty of Antarctica as well as the laborious daily tasks undertaken by the men.

Roald Amundsen's carefully designed base, Framheim, at the edge of the Great Ice Barrier. The members of the Eastern Party found Amundsen's expedition ensconced here in February 1911, a discovery that helped lead to the decision for the Eastern Party to become the Northern Party.

Amundsen generously offered to share his facilities with the members of the British expedition, should they wish to winter at the Bay of Whales, but Campbell would not consider such a course, and they continued west along the Barrier hoping to find another suitable site. They could not, however, and on February 5, they made for McMurdo to report the situation to Scott and the main body of the expedition. Scott had not returned, so after taking steps to ensure he would be informed at the earliest possible moment, Campbell and his party sailed north. Both Campbell and Pennell were anxious not only to find a location in which the newly redesignated Northern Party could winter, but also for the ship to leave before it became too late in the season to escape the ice.

In mid-February, Campbell and the five men in his charge were left at Cape Adare, where, close to Borchgrevink's old hut, they built one of their own. Perhaps it was just as well for their own peace of mind as they worked that they could have no inkling of the fact that before they were to be reunited with the rest of the expedition they were to experience two difficult winters, enduring in one of them some of the most difficult survival conditions in the history of Antarctic exploration.

Scott, meanwhile, had taken his party south with the intention of setting up several depots at intervals along the Barrier. These were to be stocked with sledging rations, oil for cooking, and food for the ponies and dogs. His goal was to place these depots as far out from their base as 80° S. In the early stages of the journey, the dogs performed magnificently, but the ponies showed not only the problems of their breed in such an environment, but also the ill effects of being battered by the weather and sea while aboard ship. The men had brought one set of a type of snowshoe adapted for the ponies, and these worked like a dream on the animal named Weary Willie. However, when Meares and Wilson attempted to go back to Cape Evans for more of them, they found that the sea ice had broken up, leaving them unable to reach their base.

The party headed south and east, establishing depots at what they named Safety Camp, and then Corner Camp. This was on the same longitude as Cape Crozier, and the intention was to aim directly south from there toward the Beardmore Glacier, which Shackleton's party had ascended to the Polar Plateau, thereby missing a dangerous series of crevasses on the direct route across the Barrier from McMurdo to the glacier. After being held up for three days by a blizzard, the party made its way south to 79°, where they established Bluff Depot.

Significant problems soon developed, however, as the ponies began to show serious signs of deterioration, despite having been out for less than three weeks. Oates argued that in their current condition the ponies would be unable to return to Hut Point, so the most productive plan would be to take them as far south as possible, and then to kill them and depot the meat for use the next spring by the men and dogs of the Polar Party. Scott felt this was inhumane, and refused. He sent three of the weaker ponies back with Teddy Evans and two of the men.

Shortly thereafter, distressed by the suffering of the remaining five ponies, Scott decided to leave the rest of the supplies at what they named One Ton Depot, located at 79° 29' S, some 30 miles (56 km) short of the point they had originally hoped to reach. Oates, who took a more pragmatic view of the ponies than Scott, again argued that all effort should be made to move the supplies as far south as possible, regardless of the cost to the animals. Again, Scott refused.

After they stowed the supplies, Scott, Wilson, Cherry-Garrard, and Meares began their return with the dogs, leaving Oates, Bowers, and Gran to bring back the five exhausted ponies. When the dog party reached Safety Camp, however, they found that only one of Evans's three ponies had survived the return journey. Worse yet, Atkinson, the surgeon who had been left behind on the outward journey with a foot injury, had returned to Hut Point, where he had found a letter from Campbell telling of the discovery of Amundsen. He passed the letter to an angry and worried Scott, who was made even more frustrated by being on the Barrier with no way back to base until the sea froze over again. For the first time, it became obvious to Scott that time was not on his side and that he was now in a race for the Pole.

On April 13, 1911, having spent about a month at Hut Point waiting for the ice of McMurdo Sound to refreeze and allow them to return to Cape Evans, Scott and his men—a motley party if ever there was one—returned to their base. Those returning included both members of the depot-laying party and Taylor's first Western Party, which had engaged in a geological survey in the Western Mountains.

While Scott was still weighing his options regarding the Norwegian threat, Oates and company arrived at Safety Camp with all five ponies, but that very night Weary Willie died. This emphasized the fact that Scott would have to allow for better conditions for the remaining ponies the next spring, meaning that he would require a later start than originally planned, which in turn, he feared, would give Amundsen an even greater head start than the 60-mile (111-km) advantage he already had. He decided, however, that "the proper, as well as the wiser, course for us is to proceed exactly as though this had not happened."

In the meantime, however, the party needed to reach the safety of Hut Point, and Meares and Wilson returned with the dog teams while Bowers, Cherry-Garrard, and Petty Officer Tom Crean continued with the remaining four ponies. After a day of exhausting and difficult travel, near the edge of the Barrier, the three camped on what proved to be unstable ice. They awoke, according to Bowers, to find: "We were in the middle of a floating pack of broken-up ice." One of the ponies had already disappeared, and while Crean raced back to Scott and Oates for help, Bowers and Cherry-Garrard desperately tried to get the other three ponies back to the Barrier. But although the men eventually reached safety, and were able to bring one pony with them, the other two ponies fell in the water, where Oates and Bowers ultimately had to kill them with pickaxes to prevent them from being devoured alive by killer whales.

Not only had Scott's party lost six of their ponies, but the men now found themselves cut off from Cape Evans. They could do nothing but move into the old *Discovery* Hut, where on March 15, they were joined by Taylor's party returning from the Western Mountains. The hut was inadequately supplied and organized for so many men, contributing to the frustrations of an already tense period. Everyone was anxious to return to Cape Evans—which now seemed a virtual oasis in their memories—and almost immediately upon the formation of the new sea ice, Scott and Evans led parties those final few miles back north. They arrived at their base on April 13, only 10 days before the sun rose for the last time, presaging a winter that for some of them would be colder, darker, and more terrible than anything they had ever experienced.

Winter at Cape Evans

Although the disappearance of the Sun mostly confined the members of the British expedition to Cape Evans, the area within and around the hut became a hive of activity. A vast array of scientific observations was made, most notably by the brilliant meteorologist Dr. George "Sunny Jim" Simpson. Part of the hut was designated as the scientists' workshop—over-generously called "laboratories"—where studies of zoology, parasitology, physics, and geology were conducted. Next to this area was the 6 by 8 foot (1.8 by 2.4 m) darkroom where Ponting not only carried out much of his work, but also slept, in company with the constant smell of photographic chemicals.

In addition to the all-important scientific program, there was a large amount of work to be done both to prepare for the spring's sledging journeys and simply to exist, day to day, in such a hostile environment. But all activities were not solely devoted to the completion of tasks; the members of the expedition found time to enjoy themselves as well. Special dinners were held whenever a suitable occasion allowed, and birthdays in particular were celebrated with great gusto. Midwinter Day, on June 22, was the highlight of the season, and was treated in the same manner as Christmas.

A Sunday service was held each week, and a variety of musical instruments had been brought south, including a pianola on which Debenham and Cherry-Garrard particularly excelled, and a banjo that Ponting played regularly (despite Griffith Taylor's comment that only Ponting was a worse musician than himself). Cherry-Garrard served as editor of the *South Polar Times*, an expedition magazine that was continued from its original appearance on Scott's first expedition. Scott also introduced a series of evening lectures, which proved not only valuable but exceptionally popular: Scott presented his plans for the following spring and summer; Wilson talked about painting, drawing, and birds; Oates taught the men how to take care of the ponies; and the scientists each discussed their specific areas of expertise.

Perhaps the favorite of these evening talks, however, were those given by Ponting, who accompanied them with showings of his exquisite lantern slides that had been taken all over the world. "Ponting would have been a great asset to our party if only on account of his lectures," Scott wrote in his diary, "but his value as a pictorial recorder of events becomes daily more apparent. No expedition has ever been illustrated so extensively."

Indeed, although his duties seemed on the surface physically light in comparison to those of many members of the expedition—who complained that he was simply doing photographic work while they were hauling materials ashore and building the hut—few worked harder or longer than Ponting. No aspect of the expedition or the environment escaped his cameras, still or moving, whether it was the natural beauty of the Antarctic, the laborious daily tasks of the men, the life of the dogs, ponies, and wildlife, or the preparations for the great sledging journeys. And photographing, developing, or printing in

One corner of the hut at Cape Evans (left) was allotted to the scientific staff to aid them in their work. One of the busiest members of the expedition was the biologist Nelson, shown here in his "biological laboratory."

the dark, freezing conditions of the Antarctic were no simple tasks. Few comments are more illustrative of the difficulties that could be encountered than an example given in *The Great White South*: "On another occasion, my tongue came into contact with the metal part of one of my cameras, whilst moistening my lips as I was focusing. It froze fast instantaneously; and to release myself I had to jerk it away, leaving the skin of the end of my tongue sticking to my camera, and my mouth bled so profusely that I had to gag it with a handkerchief."

The man who was nicknamed "Ponco" by the other expedition members expected the subjects of his photographs to give just as great an effort as he did. He could be very annoying in demanding the men hold poses for an extended period of time, particularly during periods of little light and great cold. "The photographer Ponting is an abominable nuisance," the physicist Wright wrote, "we have to be posing the whole time for his cinematograph... There are two of the men, Levick and Meares, [who] are always being photographed. I have not yet discovered whether they like it or are merely more obliging than the rest of us." Ponting's insistence on such cooperation led Griffith Taylor to invent a new verb for him: "to pont," meaning "to pose, until nearly frozen, in all sorts of uncomfortable positions."

Nevertheless, throughout the year in which Ponting was in the Antarctic, he had Scott's full blessing and cooperation. Scott was hoping to use both Ponting's photographs and his moving film to publicize the expedition and to help contribute to its coffers. In fact, Ponting would only find out when he returned to England that the rights to his photographs had been sold without his knowledge.

Music and entertainment were important parts of expedition life (above). Meares poses at the pianola, although only Cherry-Garrard and Debenham had any genuine skill on the instrument. Ponting played the banjo (badly) and sang.

In the middle of the winter of 1911, three men made the trip to Cape Crozier that was later immortalized as "the worst journey in the world." From left: Birdie Bowers, Edward Wilson, and Apsley Cherry-Garrard shortly before their departure to study the incubation of Emperor penguins and to collect some of their eggs. The journey turned into a nightmare, and the three men were lucky to return alive.

Two of Ponting's most famous photographs were of the members of a party that made a sledging trip during that winter, an excursion that has since become immortalized as "the worst journey in the world." Ever since Scott's first expedition, Wilson had wanted to make a winter visit to the Emperor penguin colony at Cape Crozier, in order to study the incubation of the birds and to collect their eggs. It was his hope that studying the Emperor penguin embryos would establish that a link existed between birds and dinosaurs, and he wanted to test theories connecting their feathers to reptilian scales. The inability to land and establish base near Cape Crozier meant that the only way to obtain the eggs necessary for the study was to make a sledge journey there in the middle of winter, soon after they had been laid.

Thus, on the morning of June 27, Wilson, Bowers, and Cherry-Garrard set off on the 58-mile (107-km) trip to the Emperor penguin colony on Cape Crozier. They knew from the outset that their journey would be brutally difficult, involving as it did hauling food and equipment on two sledges that totaled 757 pounds (343 kg) in weight, traveling over rough ice, in the dark, and experiencing some of the coldest temperatures on Earth.

Crossing Ross Island directly was impossible because of the presence of Mount Erebus, so the party went south past Cape Armitage, onto the Great Ice Barrier, and then turned northeast. Once on the Barrier, the temperatures became even colder, soon dropping to -56°F (-49°C). But that was just the beginning. At such low temperatures they could not budge the sledges on the rough surface of the Barrier, so they had to relay, hauling first one sledge and then returning for the other, dropping their progress to little better than a crawl. But even worse than the brutally hard work during the day was the time they spent in their sleeping bags at night. They froze, they shivered, their bodies cramping from the ice that continuously formed on the bags, both during the day when they were on the sledge and at night as they lay inside them.

Horrifically, the temperatures plummeted even further, reaching a low of -77°F (-61°C) on July 5, and at times not rising above -60°F (-51°C) at even the warmest time of the day. But somehow the three men struggled on, reaching their goal on July 15. Here, on a slope above the penguin colony, they built a small camp consisting of their tent and a stone igloo, the roof of which was a piece of canvas.

On July 20, they made a tortuous descent to the penguin colony, killed three penguins so that they could use the blubber to supplement their limited heating oil, and collected five eggs, two of which were broken on the climb back to the igloo. But their plans to collect more eggs were terminated when a gale made the conditions outside impossible. As they huddled in their igloo, an exceptionally strong gust blew their tent away. Knowing they could not survive the return journey without it, the three hurried out into the blizzard, but it was gone. Yet, as desperate as their situation was, it soon became worse, when their canvas roof was also destroyed by the wind. The three men retired to their icy sleeping bags to pray, sing hymns, and hope for salvation.

Wilson, Bowers, and Cherry-Garrard after struggling into Cape Evans on August 1. Their journey of 116 miles (215 km) had taken them 36 days, a more horrific period than any of them previously believed possible. As Ponting wrote: "Their looks haunted me for days."

When the gale died down, they had no choice but to search for the tent, and remarkably, Bowers found it about a quarter of a mile away. They quickly set out for home. The journey was no easier than on the way out, but the three men persevered, and on July 31 they reached Hut Point. The next night, after pushing themselves beyond what they believed they could do, they arrived at Cape Evans, where they had to be pulled forcefully out of their clothes, which had long since frozen in place on their bodies. Their journey had taken them 116 miles (215 km) in 36 days, but they had been perhaps the harshest, most demanding days in the history of Antarctic exploration. Ponting took the famous picture of the three men around the table immediately following their return—such a contrast with the sturdy, confident image he had taken at their departure on June 27—and he later wrote: "their faces bore unmistakable evidence of the terrible hardships they had endured. Their looks haunted me for days."

The Push to the Pole

On November 1, Scott and nine of his comrades, leading 10 ponies, departed from Cape Evans on the first stage of their journey toward the South Pole. Guiding them were the tracks of the two motor sledges, which had left base on October 24, hauling three sledges each and loaded with food, fuel, and equipment. Scott's orders to Teddy Evans, in command of the motor sledges, had been to proceed to Corner Camp, on to One Ton Depot, and thence due south to 80° 30' S, where they would rendezvous with Scott's pony party. Meares and Demetri were to follow Scott

A map of Scott's route on his journey to the South Pole, showing where he and his colleagues camped each night. It also marks the location where each supporting party turned back, and where the members of the Polar Party died.

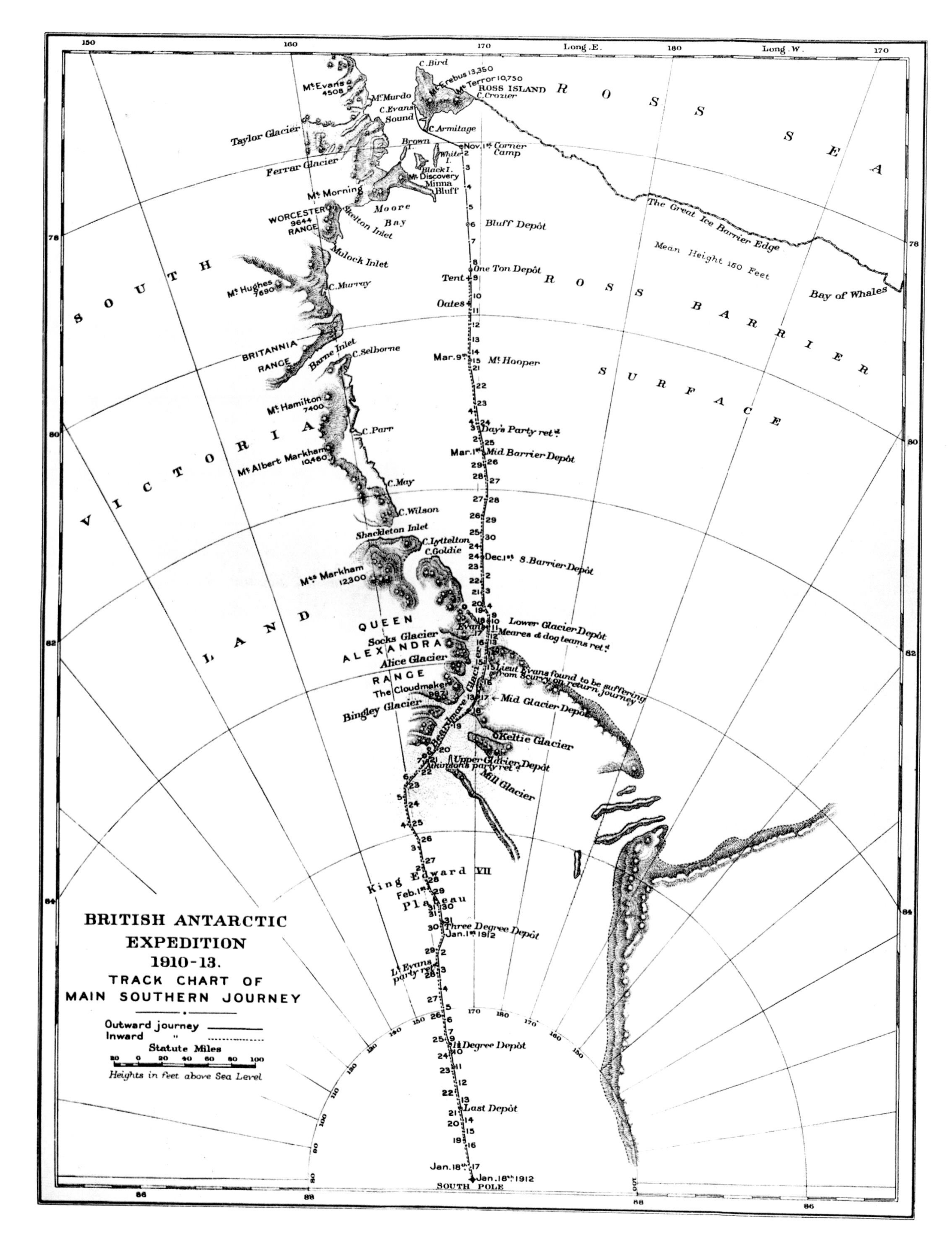

later, with 23 dogs hauling two sledges. Initially, Demetri took Ponting to the edge of the Barrier, so that he could use his cinematograph to take film of the men on their journey south with the ponies.

The procession, which ultimately numbered 16 men, 10 ponies, and 23 dogs, did not last long in its planned form, however. On November 4, before they even reached Corner Camp, the pony leaders passed one of the motor sledges, which was irretrievably broken down and abandoned. Two days later, Scott's party found the remains of the abandoned second motor sledge. Evans and his three companions—Day, Lashly, and the steward F. J. Hooper—had moved ahead taking the most valuable of the supplies from the motor sledges by man-hauling. The experiment with modern technology had proven a failure, as Oates grumpily noted after a gloomy conversation with Meares: "We both damned the motors. 3 motors at £1,000 each, 19 ponies at £5 each, 32 dogs at 30/– each. If Scott fails to get to the Pole, he jolly well deserves it."

Captain Scott and some of the members of the Polar Party and the support party pose in front of Mount Erebus during the early stages of the Southern Journey.

The unhappiness of Oates was brought about not only by the failure of the motors, but by the poor condition of the ponies—something he had regularly commented on since he had first seen them in New Zealand. He also observed the comparative ease with which Meares and Demetri brought the vibrant dog team into camp each day. It quickly became obvious that the dogs, which many of the expedition members had dismissed as a virtual irrelevancy, were the most efficient form of transport in the Antarctic environment. But with less than a quarter of the number of dogs that Amundsen had at his disposal, it was too late to do anything about it. Meanwhile, Scott made the decision that no attempt would be made to take the ponies up the Beardmore Glacier. Only enough fodder would be taken to get them to its foot, where any remaining would be killed.

On November 21, the three elements of the Southern Party were united, when pony and dog teams arrived at the point where Teddy Evans had been instructed to meet them. This became known as the Mount Hooper Depot (after Frederick Hooper, one of Evans's team) in ironic honor of the monstrous cairn that Evans and his comrades had built there while waiting for the others to arrive.

The daily progress now spread across the Barrier, as five separate starts were made after each night's camp. Evans's man-hauling team left two to three hours before those leading the ponies, who departed in three teams, based on the condition of their four-legged companions. Finally, several hours after the last of the ponies had gone, Meares, Demetri, and the dogs set out. Three days after the start of this pattern, the first pony was shot, and its leader, the surgeon Atkinson, joined the man-hauling team. At the same point, Day and Hooper were sent back to Cape Evans with a sledge and two sick dogs.

On November 26, the Mid-Barrier Depot was established at 81° 35' S. Two days after this the man-hauling team received a very welcome helping hand when Wright, the physicist, joined them after his pony was put down. The next afternoon, they passed Scott's original farthest south, which he had set almost nine years before. Not only was this an emotional and psychological boost for them all, but also they began receiving the physiological benefits from eating the pony meat—which added essential vitamins that the pre-prepared pemmican, biscuit, and other elements of their normal diet did not provide.

By early December, five of the 10 ponies had been shot, but despite heavy snow, which had slowed the progress of the remaining ponies dreadfully, the party had crept near to The Gateway—the entrance to the Beardmore Glacier. Scott hoped that the next day would see them on the glacier itself. But it was not to be, as a warm gale blew with such ferocity that they were kept in their camp for four days. All were miserable, as the temperature rose to the point where pools of water formed around and under the tents and everyone became soaked.

When the blizzard ceased, the party moved painfully forward to The Gateway. But the terrible storm had taken virtually all of the strength out of the ponies, which had to be flogged to keep moving. That night, at what was named "Shambles Camp," the remaining ponies were killed. The act brought a strange sense of relief to many of the party, their thoughts being recorded by Wilson, when he wrote: "Thank God the horses are now all done with and we begin the heavier work ourselves."

When Amundsen and his fellow Norwegians—Olav Bjaaland, Helmer Hanssen, Sverre Hassel, and Oscar Wisting—arrived in the region of the South Pole, they made many careful observations to assure themselves that they had reached the Pole. Here they take readings at the Pole, the Norwegian flag beside them.

That work began on December 10, although the three new man-hauling units were not totally on their own until Meares and Demetri had helped set up the Lower Glacier Depot the following day. Meares then turned north and sped away with the still rambunctious dogs. The three man-hauling teams, of four men each, comprised Scott, Wilson, Oates, and Petty Officer Edgar Evans; Teddy Evans, Atkinson, Wright, and Lashly; and Bowers, Cherry-Garrard, and Petty Officers Crean and Keohane. Almost immediately the second group began to show more signs of exhaustion than the other two, but this was natural as all four men had been pulling for a considerable length of time already, while the others had only been leading the ponies.

The men now engaged in harder work than most of them had imagined possible, slogging their way ahead with 700 to 800 pounds (318 to 363 kg) per sledge, up a ceaseless grade that would prove to be about 105 miles (195 km) long and would rise eventually to more than 10,000 feet (3,048 m) above sea level. On December 13, they pulled until 7:00 in the evening but managed only 4 miles (7.4 km) for the day. Three days later, conditions had not improved much, and Scott was beginning to show concern in his diary. "We must push on all we can, for we are now 6 days behind Shackleton," he wrote, mentioning, as he did frequently, the ghostly rival against whose timetable in 1908–09 he seemed always to compare his efforts.

It was ironic that Scott seemed more concerned with Shackleton than with Amundsen. The latter was now far to the south. On December 7, while Scott and his companions were trapped in their tents during the storm, Amundsen and his team, skiing across the Polar Plateau, had also thought of Shackleton. That day, they had surpassed his farthest south—an achievement which they rejoiced while giving honor to their predecessors. "We did not pass that spot," wrote Amundsen, "without according our highest tribute of admiration to the man, who—together with his gallant companions—had planted his country's flag so infinitely nearer to the goal than any of his precursors. Sir Ernest Shackleton's name will always be written in the annals of Antarctic exploration in letters of fire."

And so, indeed, would Amundsen's. For at the very moment Scott wrote about being behind Shackleton's pace, Amundsen and his four fellow Norwegians—Olav Bjaaland, Helmer Hanssen, Sverre Hassel, and Oscar Wisting—

were at the South Pole. Two days before that, they had become the first men ever to reach it, and on December 17, they left the tent they had named Polheim in order to begin their return to civilization, having taken the prize that Scott so desperately wanted.

In the meantime, the members of the British expedition continued their slow, grinding ascent of the Beardmore. On December 21, after a particularly long and difficult march, they reached the location where they established their Upper Glacier Depot, at 85° 7' S. The next morning the four men Scott considered the weakest were sent back: Atkinson, Cherry-Garrard, Wright, and Keohane. Actually, few of the men were in particularly good shape, and Oates was feeling as poorly as any of them. He was having problems both with his old thigh wound and with his feet, about which he wrote: "They have been continually wet since leaving Hut Point and now walking along this hard ice in frozen crampons has made rather hay of them." Atkinson, who was closest to Oates on the expedition, was later to tell Cherry-Garrard that Oates had not wanted to continue, but had been unwilling to disclose this to Scott. This was typical of the time, when physical weakness was seen as something to be ashamed of and when suffering in silence was considered the duty of a brave man. Oates was undoubtedly the most stoic member of the expedition, and he was not about to reveal his inner thoughts to Scott in such a situation.

Oscar Wisting and his dog team at the South Pole. After spending two days in the vicinity of the Pole, Amundsen and his men headed back north toward Framheim—and immortality.

Scott gave Atkinson one important instruction before they parted company. Scott and Meares had quarreled before the latter had turned back, and Meares had indicated that he was going to return home on *Terra Nova*, which was likely to sail before Scott's party returned to Cape Evans. Scott now instructed Atkinson to bring the dogs south later in the season in order to meet the Polar Party on its way back. It appears that Scott had developed concerns about recrossing the vast Barrier to One Ton Depot. After having dismissed them for so long, he now saw the dogs as providing the margin of error for his return.

Meanwhile, as they crossed the upper parts of the glacier, Scott's group stayed intact, while Evans and Lashly made up a new team with Crean and Bowers. Leaving behind the Upper Glacier Depot did not mean that the eight remaining men had reached a level plain and were going to have an easy time. Their route continued uphill, on and on, for more than two weeks. Even Christmas Day did not bring a break, although they did have special meals to celebrate. Scott, who was arguably the physically most powerful of the group, seemed driven as if by demons that day, and led a particularly long and difficult march, which left even the usually imperturbable Bowers exhausted. "My breath kept fogging my glasses, and our windproofs got oppressively warm and altogether things were pretty rotten," Bowers wrote. "At last [Scott] stopped and we found we had done 14 miles. He said, 'What about fifteen miles for Christmas Day?' so we gladly went on—anything definite is better than indefinite trudging."

It was not necessarily the best strategy. Although the men did their best to keep up with their chief, they were gradually wearing out, and Bowers noted that they were all getting thinner. They were suffering from a combination of factors: lack of caloric intake, dehydration, low temperatures, and high altitude. Members of both sledging teams were having difficulties.

Scott at the time seems to have focused on the problems affecting Teddy Evans's team, and on December 31, he ordered them to depot their skis and continue on foot. In retrospect, this was a strange decision, because Scott had acknowledged that it was easier to travel on skis, and two days later he wrote, "It's been a plod for the foot people and pretty easy going for us." Why he made this decision has never been fully answered. The same night, he made his final decision about who would accompany him to the Pole.

On the morning of January 3, Scott told Teddy Evans, Crean, and Lashly that they would not be part of the final Polar Party, following which he announced a remarkable change of plans by asking Evans to return with just the two men, allowing Bowers to join the Polar Party. Under the circumstances of command, Evans could hardly refuse.

Scott's decision to proceed with five men instead of four has never been fully understood, and it has been the subject of controversy for decades. It threw out the logistical planning that had been carefully followed so far, it meant that Evans's party would be seriously undermanned on the return, and it left Scott with an extra mouth to feed and another body to cram into their already small tent. So why did Scott make such a decision? Although he may have calculated that a fifth man's strength in pulling the sledge would outweigh the difficulties such a change might bring, it appears that it was an emotional, rather impulsive decision.

There had been little doubt that Wilson, Scott's companion on his previous farthest south and his confidant, as well as one of the strongest of the party, would be selected for the final push to the Pole. Bowers, although not initially one of Scott's coterie, had proven himself invaluable as a navigator, the man in charge of stores, a tireless worker, and unquestioningly a devoted follower of "the Owner." So Wilson and Bowers being named members of the final party was no surprise. However, the selections of Oates and Edgar Evans were, in retrospect, less than logical. The choice of Oates appears to have been greatly dictated by the fact that Scott, as the leader of a naval expedition, wanted a representative of the other great service—the army—to join him at the Pole. Oates had also proven his value by his indefatigable work with the ponies, but in the later stages of the journey he had increasingly suffered from problems with his feet and from his old war wound, which had left his left leg several inches shorter than the right and had made the long journey particularly difficult. In addition, his extra work with the ponies during the journey to the Beardmore had meant that he had worked longer hours than his comrades and had missed numerous meals. He was worn down, his strength and stamina sapped, and his desire to attain the Pole was not as all-encompassing as that of several of his comrades. Oates would give the final journey everything he had, but the problem was that too much of his energy had already been expended.

One of the reasons for selecting Edgar Evans had been similar to that for Oates: Scott wanted the lower deck, as well as officers, represented at the Pole. But although Evans was a large, powerful man whose very physique gave confidence in his abilities and who had utter devotion to his leader—a feeling that was reciprocated—his drinking in recent years had undoubtedly taken a toll, and Wilson had expressed doubts about his ability to perform under stress. In fact, Wilson and Atkinson had agreed, shortly before Atkinson turned back, that Lashly—a teetotaler and non-smoker—was by far the best choice of the seamen, and it appears that Crean was in better shape than Evans as well. But Scott's personal regard for Evans seems to have influenced his decision.

Thus, on January 4, a party of five continued south. One of the problems with the change of plan had already arisen, as Bowers—having been one of the group ordered to depot their skis—was forced to plod along on his short legs while his companions had the advantage of using skis. Moreover, they soon found it took considerably longer to cook for five than for four, meaning that they would run out of fuel much more quickly. Because he was forced to keep up with the men on skis, Bowers soon found himself perpetually exhausted. And Evans began to have

On March 1, the men dragged themselves into the Mid-Barrier Depot, only to discover that there was a serious shortage of oil (much of it having evaporated), and that they would be lucky to have enough to reach the next depot. Moreover, that day, after more than two months of troubles, Oates revealed the appalling state of his badly frostbitten and now gangrenous feet. They were not his only problem. The body needs vitamin C to keep scar tissue together, and the scar on Oates's thigh, a legacy from his service in the South African War, appeared to have begun to dissolve, and the wound to reopen. The three other members of the party were also suffering from scurvy, but Oates's pain must have been truly horrific.

Yet still they crawled across the seemingly endless Barrier, all of them growing progressively weaker with Oates soon no longer being able to help pull the sledge. On March 9, they reached the Mount Hooper Depot, but to their great dismay, it had not been restocked as Scott had hoped. "Shortage on our allowance all round," he wrote. "The dogs which would have been our salvation have evidently failed." In fact, because Scott's final message had never been passed on, and he had earlier forbidden Atkinson to risk the dogs by a longer journey (wishing to preserve them for further sledging the following season), the animals had not been taken past One Ton Depot, where for six days they had been waiting with Cherry-Garrard and Demetri. In terrible conditions of low temperature and wind, the party advanced slowly, but it finally became too much for Oates. On March 15, he asked to be left behind in his sleeping bag, but his comrades would not do it, so he managed another few miles.

The memorial cross erected at Observation Hill, overlooking Hut Point and the Great Ice Barrier. Made of jarrah, an Australian hard wood, the cross is 9 feet (2.7 m) high.

But the next morning, when he woke, according to Scott, "It was blowing a blizzard. He said, 'I am just going outside and may be some time.' He went out into the blizzard, and we have not seen him since… We knew that poor Oates was walking to his death, but though we tried to dissuade him, we knew it was the act of a brave man and an English gentleman. We all hope to meet the end with a similar spirit, and assuredly the end is not far."

It was not. Despite Scott's own feet now having become severely frostbitten, the three men staggered on to a point only 11 miles (20 km) south of One Ton Depot. But there a severe blizzard blew in, halting their progress. They agreed to move after it abated, but it continued and as the three weak men ran out of their remaining food and strength, all they could do was await the end in their tent.

Before he died—it is thought to have been on March 29, although that is uncertain—Scott's last major act was to write a series of letters and a message to the public, justifying his decisions and the manner in which the expedition had been run. Despite all of the difficulties they had faced, and their approaching end, he was still able to state straightforwardly that: "for my own sake I do not regret this journey, which has shown that Englishmen can endure hardships, help one another, and meet death with as great a fortitude as ever in the past."

Then, as the endless blizzard outside threatened to hide them and their achievements forever from the world, with remarkable prescience Scott wrote: "Had we lived, I should have had a tale to tell of the hardihood, endurance, and courage of my companions which would have stirred the heart of every Englishman. These rough notes and our dead bodies must tell the tale…."

CHAPTER THREE

A Tale of Endurance and Courage

Beau Riffenburgh and Liz Cruwys

A TALE OF ENDURANCE AND COURAGE

BEAU RIFFENBURGH AND LIZ CRUWYS

ON MIDWINTER DAY—JUNE 22, 1912—DR. ATKINSON, who, because of his seniority was, rather unexpectedly, the leader of the small group left wintering at Cape Evans, gave his men the opportunity to discuss what should be the priorities of the coming spring. After much deliberation, their eventual decision was unanimous. As soon as the conditions allowed, they would travel south in an effort to discover what had been the fate of their friends in the Polar Party.

It had not been an easy choice to make because, as Apsley Cherry-Garrard had indicated at the beginning of the winter, "it seemed to me unthinkable that we should leave live men to search for those who were dead." Indeed, that any such decision would even have been necessary was not something any of them had anticipated, and had been brought about by a remarkably unfortunate chain of events.

For two days, the men of the Northern Party and Terra Nova's *crew worked almost unceasingly to unload the components of the hut and the tons of stores that the party would need for a long winter at Cape Adare. Campbell and his men realized that this was not an ideal place, but time was against a change of plan or the pursuit of a better location, so they remained, knowing they would not be picked up for one year.*

The expedition included 33 Siberian sledge dogs (opposite), which were berthed on the open deck. Scott noted that the animals had the most wretched time, even in calm weather, and they regularly whined pitifully. Waves constantly broke over the bulwarks and drenched them, so that they sat with their coats sodden. One was strangled by his chain in the gale that struck shortly after the expedition sailed south from New Zealand. Another, Osman, was washed overboard by a wave, but was swept right back aboard. JANUARY 3, 1911

The 19 Manchurian ponies (above) had a miserable journey south in tiny stables located on the upper deck and under the fo'c'sle of Terra Nova*—so miserable that some did not complete the voyage. Here, Oates poses with some of his charges, for which he himself had purchased and smuggled aboard five extra tons of fodder.* 1910–1912

When Wilfred Bruce (opposite) was hired for the expedition, his vetting process had undoubtedly taken into account the fact that he was the brother of Scott's wife Kathleen. His first major task was to help Meares bring the ponies and dogs to New Zealand from Siberia. A commander in the Royal Naval Reserve, he was one of the ship's officers, sailing north as winter approached and returning south again the following spring. Besides his regular duties, he kept the zoological log for Lillie during the cruise in March–April 1911.
1910–1912

Lieutenant Harvey Rennick (left) wearing an odd combination of fashions aboard Terra Nova. *Rennick became the executive officer aboard ship once the shore parties had been dropped off.*
1910–1912

Much as cruise-ship passengers doze in the Antarctic sun today, so Terra Nova's *crew took advantage of a wind-free, sun-lit corner to nap and read. Space was evidently in short supply.*
December 1910

Because her heavy supplies put *Terra Nova* very low in the water, the pumps often had to be manned in heavy seas. All hands were expected to help, even the officers and scientific staff. This photograph was taken early in the expedition, as the presence of "Birdie" Bowers on the far left indicates.
DECEMBER 1910

On the last day of November 1910, Wilson recorded in his diary that there was a fair, light wind and that those who were sea sick "really had no reason." By noon on the following day, it was a different story. The barometer was falling and both wind and sea were rising. The wind was so strong that the topgallant sails were taken in, followed by other sails in quick succession; heavy green seas pummeled the overloaded vessel. By Friday, December 2, the steam pumps were unable to keep the stokehold free of water, and the valves became clogged. While Lashly and the leading stokers struggled with them, all hands were called to operate the hand pumps. As can be seen from this picture (opposite), the pumps were deployed in the waist of the ship, and needed to operate continually to prevent Terra Nova *from foundering.*
March 1912

The man at the wheel had to say "thank you" twice after this photograph (above) was taken, first to his friend who brought him a warm drink of Oxo and secondly to the photographer. Ponting set up the photograph to please one of the expedition's sponsors, Mr. Maltwood of the Liebig Company, which supplied Oxo and Lemco.
1910–1912

On December 9, 1910, Terra Nova entered the pack ice far north of where a disappointed Scott had hoped to meet it (above). For many of those aboard it was a totally new experience, and they clustered around the rails of the fo'c'sle as the ship progressed into this new environment.
DECEMBER 9, 1910

As the ship made her slow way through the beginning of the closely packed ice (right), the scene was one of incredible splendor. On December 9, 1910, Scott wrote in his diary: "The sky has been wonderful, with every form of cloud in every condition of light and shade; the sun has continually appeared through breaks in the cloudy heavens from time to time, brilliantly illuminating some field of pack, some steep-walled berg, or some patch of bluest sea."
DECEMBER 9, 1910

The ice along the edge of the land had broken into large pieces, but had not been blown out completely to sea when Ponting captured this scene, complete with inquisitive penguins doing the exploring rather than men.
1910–1912

Scientific work was a main priority on Scott's expedition, and meteorological and oceanographic data were collected on a daily basis. Here (right) a water bottle is lowered over Terra Nova's *side to assist in oceanographic studies of the temperature and salinity of the Antarctic waters.*
DECEMBER 17, 1910

Wilson (right) shot a number of birds and seals for his scientific work. Like all such naturalists, he had to be very careful to make certain he killed his targets, otherwise the injured animals might escape, their deaths not benefiting science. Some of Wilson's specimens are now held in the Natural History Museum in London, where they remain a valuable source of information to biologists.
1910–1912

The officers and scientists in the wardroom of Terra Nova, *which was a large, but somewhat crowded facility. The "ratings" messed separately, in true Royal Navy tradition.*

Scott can be seen at the head of the table, with Wilson two places to the right. Photographs of the King and Queen hang on the wall. 1910–1912

Terra Nova caught in a band of pack ice (opposite). It took more than 20 days and 61 tons of coal to break through to the open sea beyond the pack.
DECEMBER 13, 1910

On December 11, a Sunday, after Scott read Divine Service, all hands left the ship to exercise on the sea ice (above). Some practiced skiing, and Scott professed himself "much pleased" by their efforts.
DECEMBER 11, 1910

Ponting was intrigued by every aspect of the expedition, in this case the way in which the ship's water supplies were replenished. He later described in The Great White South *how "everyone—officers, scientists and men—set-to with a will, taking turns with the picks and shovels, and in a few hours we had shipped ten tons of ice... Thus we replenished our depleted fresh-water supply, and provided an animated scene for the kinematograph."* DECEMBER 11, 1910

The majestic Mount Erebus (above), with its summit hidden by clouds and smoke, dominates the otherwise placid setting of the shore of Ross Island. Thin wedges of ice float by calmly, in serene comparison to the awsome power of the mighty volcano and the glacial ice. JANUARY 3, 1911

Ponting took this photograph of Mount Erebus (opposite) from Back Door Bay, a small inlet at Cape Royds where Ernest Shackleton had landed much of his equipment. An intricately shaped berg formation makes for an intriguing foreground to the volcano which, Ponting wrote in The Great White South, *reminded him of Mount Fuji in Japan.* FEBRUARY 16, 1911

In this wonderful panorama, Ponting caught the different kinds of ice that proved such a challenge to this and all other Antarctic expeditions of the time.
1910–1912

Ponting was captivated by the beauty of this grotto (opposite) in the midst of an iceberg. He wrote in The Great White South *that it was "the most wonderful place imaginable. From outside, the interior appeared quite white and colourless, but, once inside, it was a lovely symphony of blue and green ... by almost incredible good luck, the entrance to the cavern framed a fine view of the* Terra Nova *lying at the ice-foot." Ponting enthused so wildly about the ice grotto's beauty that several expedition members went to see and admire it. Taylor and Wright are in the grotto here.*
JANUARY 5, 1911

Ponting's "most wonderful" grotto (left) was about a mile from the ship, and was the subject of his first photographic excursion in the region of Cape Evans. He took several photographs here, which are among the most famous of his remarkable career. Scott and Wilson both later went with him to see the grotto.
JANUARY 5, 1911

While officers, scientists, and men labored at transporting the expedition supplies from Terra Nova to land, Ponting took photographs, such as these Adélie penguins (above) with the glittering white mass of Mount Erebus looming behind them. This caused some resentment, although Ponting worked long hours and went to endless lengths to secure perfect pictures.
JANUARY 5, 1911

Skuas are fiercely protective of their eggs and young, so the parents of this chick and its unhatched siblings (above) made taking their photograph risky. But Ponting had caught the attention of killer whales during his career, so he probably did not see the skuas as a great danger.
JANUARY 6, 1911

Ponting, wearing his distinctive hat (right), waits with infinite patience for his skua subjects to pose around a seal carcass. Ponting was not the first person to use a cinematograph in the Antarctic—Eric Marshall had done so on Shackleton's British Antarctic Expedition of 1907–09—but the film Ponting made from his footage remains the classic moving picture of early Antarctic exploration.
JANUARY 7, 1911

As the unloading process continued on January 7, Ponting managed to capture one remarkable scene after another. Here (left), in one of his most famous photographs, Terra Nova *sits serene and silent in smooth pack ice, while nearer the shore the ice breaks into a jumble of crags and jetties reflected in frigid pools.*
JANUARY 7, 1911

On January 8, it was decided that Terra Nova *was too vulnerable so close to the shore, so she was moved a mile away to a safer anchorage. This meant a much longer walk across the pack ice to unload supplies. Here (above), Scott, Wilson, and Teddy Evans make the tedious journey back.*
JANUARY 9, 1911

One problem with taking ponies to the Antarctic was the amount of bulky feed they required. Bales of fodder were placed on sledges (above) and then man-hauled across the sea ice to the hut and stables. Man-hauling was something Scott was very good at, and he doubtless saw the entire landing operation as an excellent chance for the men to become accustomed to doing it.
JANUARY 1911

On January 8, 1911, Teddy Evans noted in his diary with typical British understatement: "This morning a regrettable accident took place... [right] The third and newest motor sledge was hoisted out and, while being hauled clear on to the firm ice, it broke through and sank in deep water... It was nobody's fault, as Simpson and Campbell both tested the floe first and found it quite thick and apparently good. However, there it is, in about 100 fathoms of water."
JANUARY 8, 1911

B.A.E.
SHIPS
PARTY
COLMAN'S
WHOLE
WHEAT MEAL

No1743
B.A.E.
SHORE PARTY
COLMAN'S
CORN-FLOUR
No.1744
B.A.E.
SHORE PARTY
COLMAN'S
CORN-FLOUR
SHORE PARTY
B.A.E.

On December 22, having established the Upper Glacier Depot, four of the remaining dozen men were "told off" by Scott and returned to base. Of these, Charles "Silas" Wright, the Canadian physicist, was perhaps the most disappointed, "rather bitterly, I fear," according to Scott. This photograph was taken on his return to Cape Evans in late January 1912.
JANUARY 29, 1912

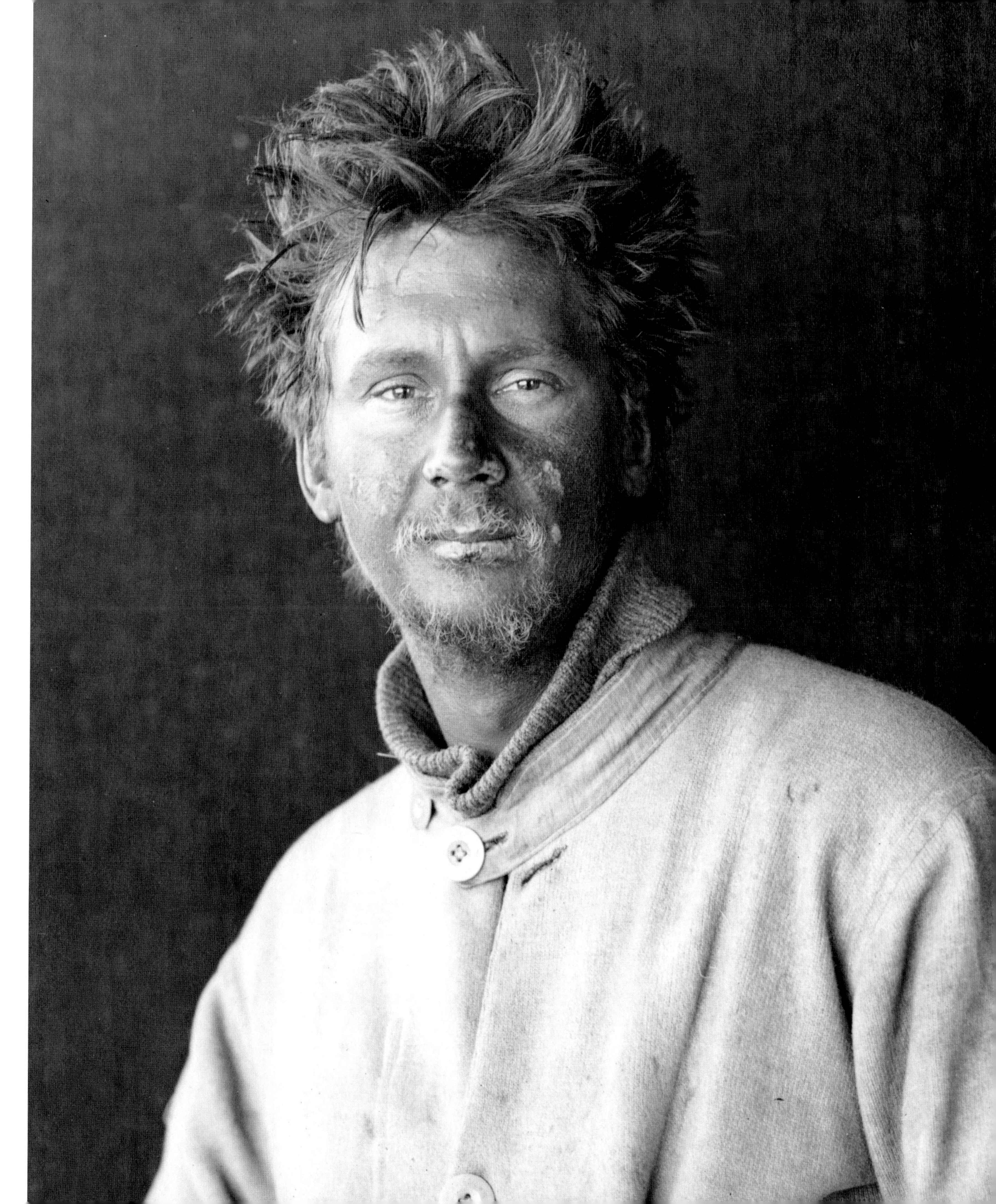

On April 13, 1911, Scott, photographed here by Ponting, returned to Cape Evans with two parties of his men from a period spent at Hut Point after having been cut off from their main base by the sea ice blowing out of McMurdo Sound.
April 13, 1911

Other members of the shore party, who had been forced to remain for weeks at Hut Point in the fall of 1911 while the sea ice refroze on McMurdo Sound, photographed by Ponting. Clockwise (from top left) are Wilson, physicist "Silas" Wright, Tryggve Gran, and Second-in-Command Teddy Evans.
APRIL 1911

One of the men who returned with Scott to Cape Evans was Griffith Taylor (left), an Australian geologist who had been in command of the First Western Party. Like his colleague Frank Debenham, Taylor was a former student of T. W. Edgeworth David, one of the most influential figures in early Antarctic geology.
APRIL 13, 1911

Two other expedition members who returned to Cape Evans on April 13 were the petty officers, Edgar Evans and Tom Crean (opposite).
APRIL 13, 1911

Taken with a telephoto lens from 70 miles (130 km) away—right across McMurdo Sound—this photograph shows the outline of Mount Lister as well as the smaller peaks in front of it. Ponting also managed to catch in his frame the dying iceberg in the foreground. The berg has grounded, and tides and waves are eroding its base.
February 10, 1911

Cape Evans had a serene, beautiful look at times, although it was much less so during the harsh winter Scott's party was to spend there. Here Ponting caught the sunlight reflecting off the water. Near the hut are many different depots of supplies and gear, which were placed wide apart to avoid the risk of fire.
1910–1912

Home for the men (opposite). Drifted snow covers the supplies in the fore-ground, while the heat of the stoves inside the hut keeps the roof relatively clear. Skis were always set upright so they would not be lost in drifted snow.
JUNE 13, 1911

Scientific observations went on all winter and Ponting was keen to capture as many activities as possible with his lens. Lieutenant Evans (above) was one of his victims, forced to pose in sub-zero temperatures until Ponting was satisfied with the result. Evans was viewing an occultation of Jupiter and he was in telephone contact with Dr. Simpson inside the hut, who was timing the observation.
JUNE 8, 1911

Throughout the winter the ponies (above) were cared for with remarkable tenderness by Oates, who had a deep affection for them even if he considered them to be of a lower quality than he would have chosen himself. In the early winter, it was already so cold that the ponies' breath condensed while Oates stood with them in companionable silence.
MAY 25, 1911

Next to the main body of the hut were the stables where the ponies were kept throughout the winter of 1911 (right). In this area was a stove that burned seal blubber rather than traditional fuel, which was saved for the main hut and for the journeys to the interior. Here, Meares and Oates sit contentedly smoking their pipes adding to the already smoky atmosphere.
MAY 26, 1911

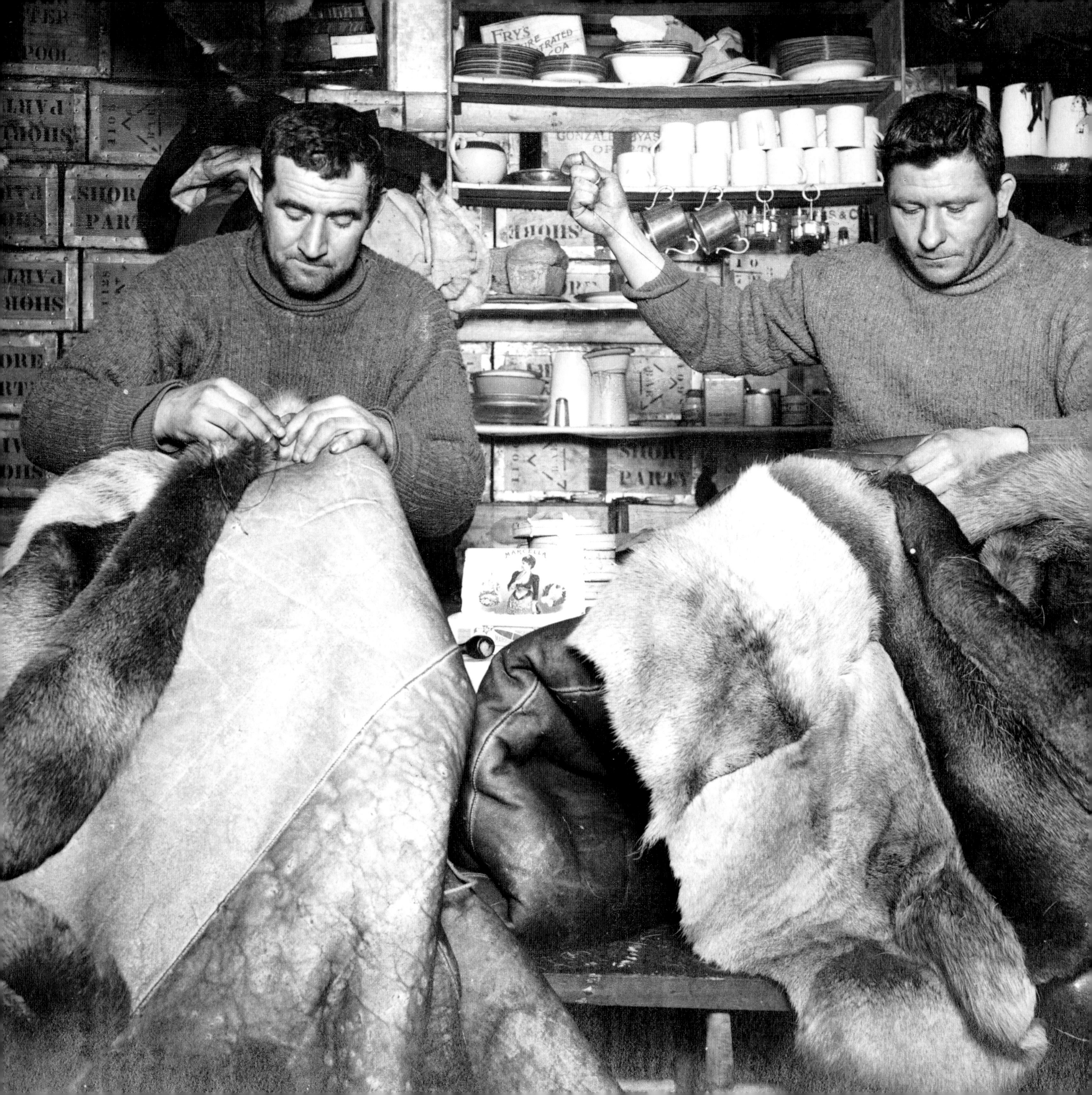
FRY'S
SHORE
PARTY

One thing the dark and cold of winter could not interfere with was the expedition's scientific program. Here (right) the two geologists with the main party at Cape Evans—Frank Debenham and Griffith Taylor—carefully engage in their scientific work.
MAY 22, 1911

Throughout the long, dark winter of 1911, the members of the expedition attempted to repair and improve the equipment they had brought with them, based on their experiences on the Barrier in January and February 1911. One of their most important tasks was mending their heavy sleeping bags. Here (opposite) two petty officers, Crean and Evans, are sewing the reindeer-skin sleeping bags.
MAY 16, 1911

Like many Royal Navy officers, Lieutenant Evans (left) had training in drafting and map-making. This allowed him to make a continuing contribution to the expedition throughout the winter.
MAY 23, 1911

Thomas Clissold (left) producing a meal in the galley. His job usually meant that he was the last man to have to worry about getting too cold. Note the Heinz tomato ketchup with its distinctive label behind Clissold's pan.
AUGUST 30, 1911

Scott had faced major problems with the cook on his first expedition, so this time he went to great lengths to find a man who would not only be an excellent cook, but would fit in with the expedition. Thomas Clissold fit the bill, and was popular as well as appreciated for his culinary skills. Among Clissold's many jobs was to keep the expedition members well supplied with fresh bread, which he baked daily (opposite).
MARCH 26, 1911

from
THIS PACKAGE CONTAINS
FOR THE
RITISH ANTARCTIC EXPEDITION, 191
S.S. "TERRA NOVA"
LYTTELTON
GELATINE
BLACK PEPPER
GILLARD'S
CHOICE
ENGLISH SOUPS
COCK A LEEKIE
HEINZ
TOMATO
SOUP
SALMON STEAK
RHUBARB
Victoria Buildings
FRY'S
MALTED COCOA
COCOA
Griffiths McAlister & Co.
LIVERPOOL
BEEF MARROWFAT
COD ROES
BACON RATIONS
RATIONS
CINNAMON
PEARL SAGO

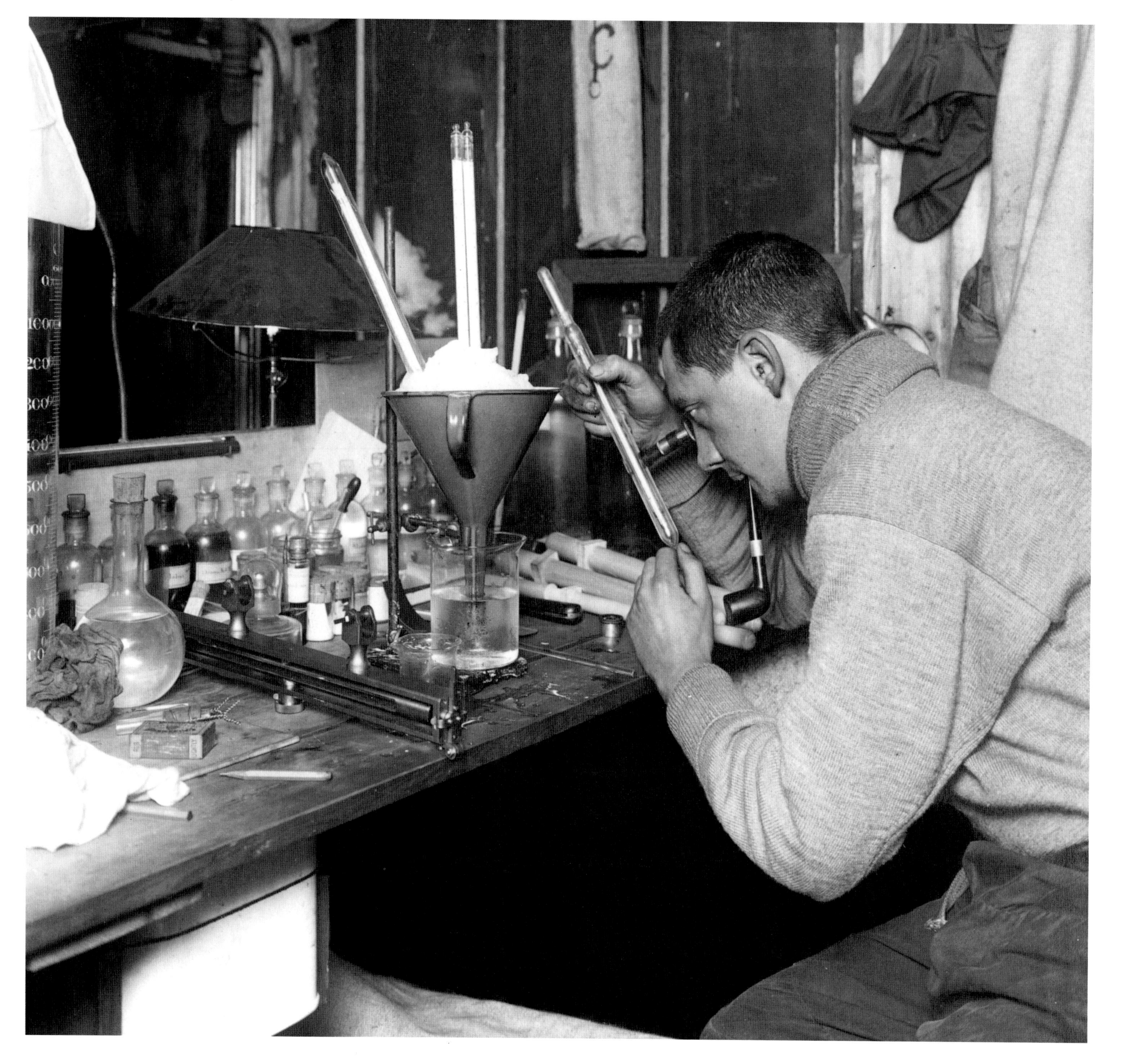

Some geological specimens needed to be polished before they could be examined microscopically (opposite). Frank Debenham, well wrapped up against the chill even inside the hut, prepares samples.
JULY 12, 1911

Scott was a great enthusiast about modern technology, and he had a telephone cable run all the way from Cape Evans to Hut Point (right), making use of the new contraption for communication about scientific observations. Shortly before he left on the Southern Journey, he noted in his diary, "This morning Simpson has just rang up. He says the motors are in difficulties with the surface. The trouble is just that which I noted as alarming on Monday—the chains slip on the very light covering of hard ice."
JULY 14, 1911

As on Scott's first expedition, an in-house magazine entitled The South Polar Times *was produced by this expedition. Cherry-Garrard (above) was editor, following in the footsteps of Shackleton, who had been so on the* Discovery *Expedition almost a decade before. Day bound the volume in a cover of venesta wood and sealskin. The first issue, released on Midwinter's Day, included a geological article by Taylor and a plan of the forthcoming Southern Journey by Scott, as well as poems and lighter, more humorous pieces.*
AUGUST 30, 1911

One of the most impressive tasks performed during the winter at Cape Evans was masterminded by Petty Officer Patrick Keohane. He is shown (opposite) putting the final touches to his accurately proportioned and extremely intricate model of Terra Nova.
AUGUST 10, 1911

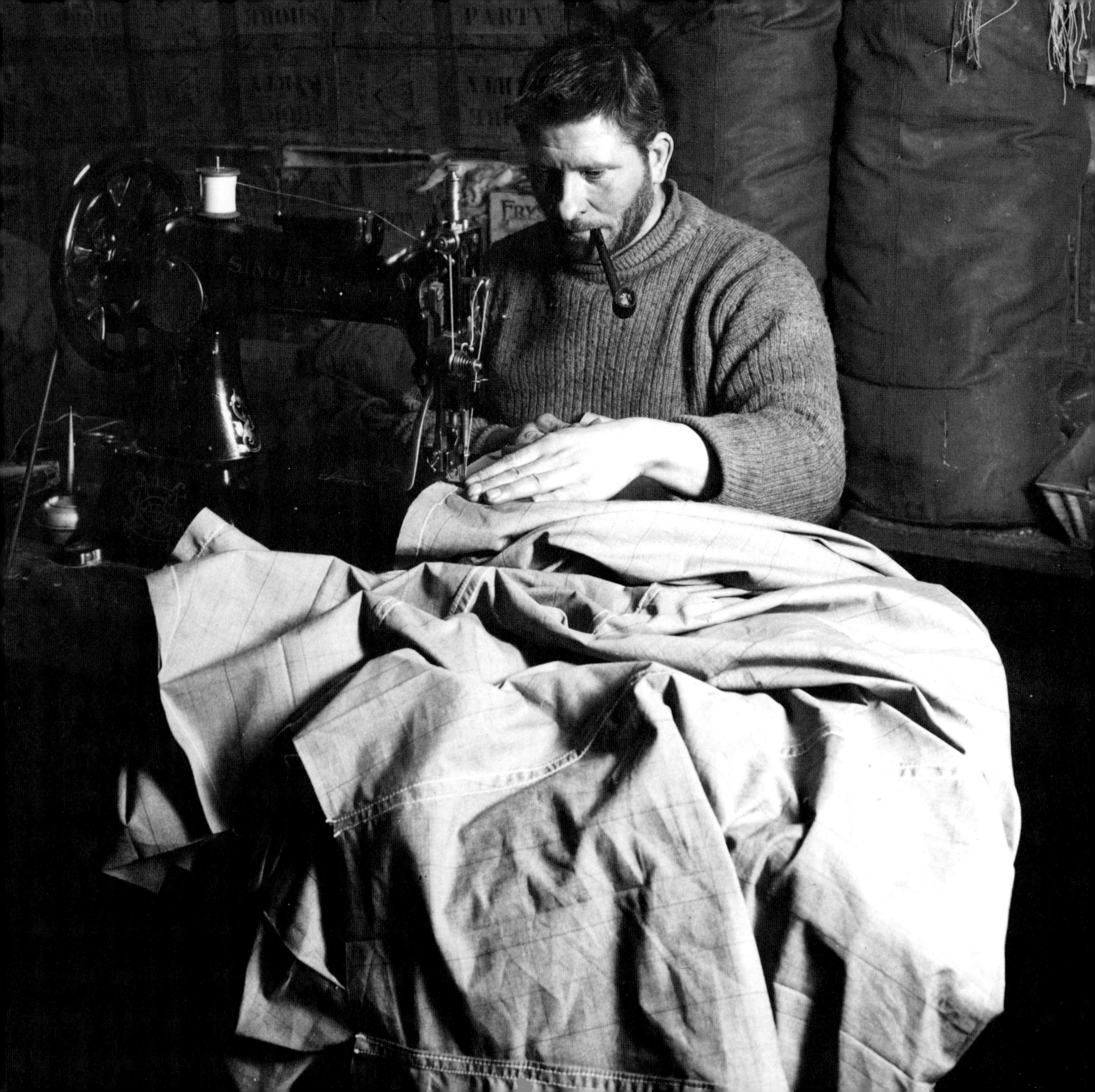
PARTY
FRY

Petty Officer Evans is often remembered for his remarkable physical strength and ability. However, he was a man of many talents, as shown by his work (opposite) at the sewing machine in overhauling the sleeping bags and canvas tents for the Polar Party.
1910–1912

Dr. George Simpson (above) had tried unsuccessfully to join Scott's first expedition. His quality as a scientist was proved beyond a shadow of a doubt on this venture, as he made a series of meteorological observations that are still used as a basis of comparison today. Here he is at work in the hut where magnetic data were recorded.
JANUARY 5, 1912

FRY'S

The "tenements" (left) were a chaotic cluster of five bunk beds and belongings that were home to Cherry-Garrard (left), Bowers (standing), Oates (middle), Meares (top right), and Atkinson (bottom right). The scene can still be viewed in Scott's hut, with socks drying at the end of the bed and harnesses hanging in a jumble, almost as if their owners had "just gone outside" and are expected to return soon.
OCTOBER 9, 1911

Ponting gave several winter lectures, including one on his photographic work in Japan (above), using glass slides from his book In Lotus-Land: Japan. *As Scott wrote in his diary, "To-night Ponting gave us a charming lecture on Japan with wonderful illustrations of his own. He is happiest in his descriptions of the artistic side of the people, with which he is in fullest sympathy. So he took us to see the flower pageants... His descriptions were well given and we all of us thoroughly enjoyed our evening."*
OCTOBER 16, 1911

Ponting couldn't get enough of Castle Berg (opposite). In The Great White South *he wrote that in the sunlight, "the berg became of such gleaming beauty that even the most unimpressionable members of our community felt the influence of its spell. There was but one opinion concerning it amongst us—that it was the most wonderful iceberg ever reported in the Polar regions."*
SEPTEMBER 17, 1911

Another view of Castle Berg (above), this time taken by flashlight in June 1911, the middle of winter. Ponting masterfully captures the darkness and shadows, which set it off in a mysterious and captivating manner.
JUNE 4, 1911

Scott, in the center of the photograph, and other expedition members prepare for their departure on an early stage of the Southern Journey. Ponting accompanied his colleagues as far as the Great Ice Barrier, where he said what proved to be a final farewell to Scott and the other four members of the final Polar Party. 1910–1912

At the start of the Southern Journey, Day's motor sledge passes Inaccessible Island (above and top). Teddy Evans, who was in command of the motor sledges, guides Day's sledge through some difficult terrain.
NOVEMBER 1911

The members of the Second Western Party had been waiting for nearly a month to be picked up by Terra Nova *when they finally saw the ship. They began to race toward her (right), attempting to pull their sledge across some two miles (3.7 km) of cracking ice floes. Four men came out to meet the party and helped haul the sledge over the floes, which were rapidly breaking up and floating northward in great fragments. When their way was slowed by the increasing distance between the floes, the ship butted a large floe toward the ice they were on and held it there long enough for the men to get the sledge across to safety. This photograph shows the party gathering speed to propel their sledge across a gap between floes.*
MARCH 1911

Clissold and Anton Omelchenko torment an Emperor penguin that had the misfortune to wander into their hands (above).
1910–1912

Ponting was delighted when he found this Adélie penguin rookery placed artistically before Mount Erebus (right). Sometimes thought of as the "classic" penguin, Adélies are found in large numbers around much of the Antarctic continent. This particular rookery is at Cape Royds.
November 27, 1911

A skua lands next to a dead penguin to feed (opposite). Skuas are predators and scavengers, as happy taking fresh prey such as penguin chicks as they are feasting on a corpse. Skuas are careful not to take on adult penguins, which have powerful beaks and wings. Any injury that prevents a skua from flying will almost certainly result in its death, particularly if it cannot fly north at the end of the summer. Behind the birds, the ponies, tethered to each other to prevent them from running away, nose the snow in a futile hunt for a blade of grass below it.
1910–1912

Weddell seals (above and right) are true Antarctic mammals in that they remain far south even when the sea is covered in ice. They do, however, need access to leads, polynias, or breathing holes in order to come up for air. Weddell seals make breathing holes by gouging the ice from below with their strong and very hard teeth. The sharp, grating sound of enamel on rock-hard ice is a common sound near these holes in winter, as the seals' survival often depends on keeping them from freezing over. Such activities are hard on their teeth, which gradually wear down to gum level. When a seal reaches the point where it can no longer keep its holes open, it may well drown, a process known as "dental death."
1910–1912

Seals hauled out at the foot of the towering Church Berg. Some larger icebergs were semi-permanent features of the expedition's landscape, having become trapped in winter sea ice and, sometimes, aground in shallow water.
DECEMBER 29, 1911

"The warm [sun], beating on [icebergs], melted [the] snow, so that white ice only remained, tinged with the delicate hues of aquamarine and tourmaline; whilst every crack was turquoise and each deeper fissure azure," wrote Ponting in The Great White South.
DECEMBER 29, 1911

In fine weather, the crow's nest (opposite) was a popular place, particularly following the first sighting of the ice. It was less pleasant in high winds, when the strong cold winds cut through even the thickest clothing. When the ship was navigating through the pack ice, it was essential to have someone in the crow's nest to point the helmsman toward the best leads and open water.
1910–1912

The Ship's Crew

After spending the winter in warmer climes, Terra Nova *returned to the Antarctic in January 1912, bringing supplies, a passage home for some of those who had wintered, and replacements for some of the staff.*
1912

The men in the front row of this photograph (above), taken on the return to New Zealand, are (from left): James Skelton (AB), Thomas McLeod (AB), Petty Officer Arthur Bailey, Petty Officer Robert Forde, and Joseph Leese (AB).

The back row includes (from left): Fireman Angus McDonald, William McDonald (AB), 2nd Engineer William Horton, Stoker William Burton, Stoker Robert Brissenden, Fireman Thomas McGillion, Petty Officer Frederick Parsons, Stoker Edward McKenzie, Petty Officer William Heald, the groom Anton Omelchenko, Steward W. H. Neale, the cook Thomas Clissold, Leading Seaman Albert Balson, Petty Officer John Mather, Mortimer McCarthy (AB), and Leading Shipwright Francis Davies.

Messrs. J. S. Fry & Sons, the famous chocolate manufacturer, was another of the expedition's suppliers. Here (right) in another of Ponting's carefully choreographed shots, three crew members wrapped warmly in matching polar gear are about to enjoy their chocolate allowance. Fry & Sons provided the expedition with "cocoa, sledging and fancy chocolate—delicious comforts, excellently packed and always in good condition." 1910–1912

To get south, Terra Nova *(opposite) had to sail through the Roaring Forties, the Furious Fifties, and the Screaming Sixties. Passing through these latitudes could be very uncomfortable for the inexperienced sailor and even for a very experienced seaman.* 1912

Cape Crozier (opposite), home to the Emperor penguin colony which so interested Edward Wilson that he, Birdie Bowers, and Apsley Cherry-Garrard made an expedition in mid-winter to it to study the birds' incubation patterns and to gather some of their eggs. The sea and ice conditions at Cape Crozier, located at the eastern end of Ross Island immediately adjacent to the Great Ice Barrier, made it impossible for Scott's party to land there.
JANUARY 3, 1911

Ponting's moving picture film Ninety Degrees South *contained footage filmed from the ship (left) of whales that approached* Terra Nova, *including both killer whales (orcas) and the great Baleen whales that were so attractive to the whaling industry. Whalers had been dipping ever further south in their quest for unexploited populations for some time, although it was only after the 1920s that serious damage was done. Blue whales, in particular, suffered from over-hunting, and many biologists fear the plunder was too great to allow the stocks to recover. Only the very fortunate visitor to the Antarctic will glimpse one of these magnificent animals today, whereas at the time Ponting was filming them, their numbers were estimated to be as high as 240,000.*
1910–1912

CHAPTER FOUR

ANTARCTIC PIONEER

H.J.P ("Douglas") Arnold

ANTARCTIC PIONEER

H.J.P ("DOUGLAS") ARNOLD

As HERBERT GEORGE PONTING PURSUED HIS CAREER as a talented professional photographer in many lands in the years up to World War I, and capped those experiences in Antarctica during Scott's *Terra Nova* Expedition, it would have been understandable if, during those challenging and sometimes dangerous moments, his mind had not turned briefly to his more comfortable beginnings in the English West Country of the later Victorian years. Indeed, if life had mirrored paternal aspirations, Herbert would have been employed in banking rather than risking life and limb covering wars for the news media or being attacked by killer whales.

Herbert Ponting in his early 20s, around the time that he unsuccessfully tried to make a living at fruit farming and mining in the United States.

His background was certainly not lacking in color—at least on his mother's side. Mary Sydenham came from rich West Country stock, which could boast of Sir Francis Drake in the family line as well as a later physician, Thomas Sydenham, accorded the title of "Father of English Medicine." The Pontings were reputedly of Huguenot extraction and Herbert's grandfather Henry, a former pupil at the prestigious Marlborough School, became an agent to the Marquis of Ailesbury in the Savernake Forest of Wiltshire. Henry's skills were doubtless an example for his eldest son Francis—Herbert's father—who proceeded to make a mark in the world of banking at a time of great expansion. Increasingly senior management posts in various parts of the country charted his success and he was able to leave formal employment in his early fifties and devote himself to furthering his own financial interests. When he died in 1923, aged 81, his estate was worth £45,000—equivalent to some £1.3 million at today's values.

Herbert was born in Salisbury, Wiltshire, on March 21, 1870, the eldest son in a family of four boys and four girls. The family moved around the country from Salisbury to Carlisle as Francis's career developed, and they lived in a manner befitting his status. There were maids, a cook, a gardener, and a coachman, and life was very comfortable. Francis was not interested in political or public life and his work and family were the twin centers of his attention. There were musical evenings, games, and outings for the children, whose parents appear to have been firm but not dominating in the classic Victorian manner. At school none achieved any great distinction and, after leaving college, Herbert entered banking at a local branch in Liverpool. By the end of four years he was convinced that he was not cut out to follow his father's career path, and with Francis's blessing and considerable financial support set out for the west coast of the United States.

No detail has survived about the family discussions that doubtless took place before the decision was taken, or why specifically the United States was chosen. It was significant that Herbert's rejection of banking as a career seems in no way to have alienated his father, and that although some of Herbert's siblings began to be a little irked at living in the shadow of their brother's increasing fame, Francis's pride in his son steadily increased.

When he arrived in California in 1893 or 1894, however, fame and photography still lay some way in the future. Using some of the funds given to him by his father, he purchased a fruit farm, and then invested in a gold mine. A portrait taken at this time shows a rather dashing and suave individual who was doubtless popular with the ladies.

"Telephotograph of ships in San Francisco Bay" was one of Ponting's early award-winning photographs. Shot from near his home in Sausalito, the picture was honored by an award from no less a judge than the optical company Bausch & Lomb.

In June 1895, he married Mary Biddle Elliott, the daughter of a US army general, and over the next five years a daughter and a son were born. It was not too long before both the farm and the mine ran into financial difficulties, but by then Herbert had discovered photography.

He took it up seriously in 1900 when, as he wrote in *The Weekly Press* in 1910, "I had to stereograph everything I could. The beautiful stereoscopic process had a hold on me [that] … got stronger and stronger." Ponting applied himself diligently to perfecting his handling of the stereograph technique, in which a specially adapted camera takes two views simultaneously (spaced slightly apart to mimic the separation of the eyes); the resulting pair of photographs is seen through a viewer that combines them into a single, apparently three-dimensional image. Within a short time he was winning prizes for his work—a "telephotograph" of ships in San Francisco Bay shot from his home in Sausalito received recognition from the optical company Bausch & Lomb, while another, a superb shot of "Mules at a Californian Round-up," was featured at a World's Fair by Kodak. A professional photographer advised him to submit examples of his work to specialist steroscope companies. This he did successfully, being "so staggered by the prices offered that I thought this method was the best way of 'scrapping' negatives I had ever known…"

This was the beginning of more than a decade of globe-trotting. In 1901 he went on a tour of the Far East on behalf of the magazine *Leslie's Weekly* and the Universal Photo Art Company of Philadelphia. Not long after his return, Underwood & Underwood, another major publisher of stereo photographs, commissioned him to go to

The ascent of Mount Asama in Japan was one of the most harrowing episodes of Ponting's career. As he and some of the men who had hauled his equipment to the top of the volcano stood near the opening of the crater, a small eruption threw tons of rock upward, accompanied by thick sulphurous fumes. The men with him fled, and Ponting had to follow them to get back his equipment in order to return and record the scene.

Japan, and he took many photographs in Korea and Manchuria too. Then, when the Russo-Japanese War broke out in 1904, he was accredited as a war photographer to the First Japanese Army in Manchuria, working for *Harper's Weekly* and H. C. White & Co. It is impossible to establish the precise chronology of his travels after the Russo-Japanese War ended in 1905, but he was certainly in China and India in 1906–07, and back in Europe, taking mountain photographs in Switzerland and France, in 1908.

Spain, Portugal, Russia, Java, and Burma were other countries to which he was sent on assignment, and the list of magazines and periodicals in which his photographs appeared, both in Britain and the United States, was impressive. It included *Harper's*, *Century*, *World's Work*, *Strand*, *Wide World*, *Metropolitan*, *Cosmopolitan*, *Sunset*, *Pearson's*, *Leslie's Weekly*, *Sphere*, *Illustrated London News*, and *Graphic*. His work was featured in *L'Illustration* and other Continental weeklies, and he was a particularly frequent contributor to *Country Life*.

Often Ponting contributed well-researched articles as well as photographs to the magazines. Where this was not the case, it is now difficult to assess the full body of his work because the captions to the pictures would simply credit the photographic agency, making attribution to a particular photographer difficult. But the power of his work was obvious. The "seeing eye" is a convenient phrase to describe an inherent skill, but Ponting had developed this strongly in his landscape and pictorial work, and his portraits, particularly of craftsmen at work, had considerable impact. Whether tramping up to the top of a mountain over and over again (wielding a heavy camera and large glass-plate negatives) until the conditions were just right, facing acute discomfort, sometimes danger, to get a photograph, or developing negatives to extract the maximum detail and quality from them, he became the complete and dedicated self-taught professional. Ponting had no time for theoretical and often vituperative

No matter where he went, Ponting took a massive armory of equipment to make certain he could take the best photograph possible. Here, he stands atop a 10-foot (3-m) stepladder hauled all the way to the top of a Japanese volcano to obtain just the right angle.

In Japan, Ponting was awed by the mystical power of Mount Fuji. He photographed the volcano from many different angles. When he finally ascended it, he found a view of "indescribable beauty," as the clouds were transfigured into an amazing array of colors and shades as the sun sank through and below them.

arguments about what photography was or was not, or for debates about its status as an art form. Driven at some times by what the market required, and at others by what the imagination directed, Ponting simply sought to always make his images the best. A contemporary distinguished portrait photographer and friend, E. O. Hoppé, perhaps best summed up Ponting's work when he described him as a perfectionist and his own fiercest critic—"the supreme pictorial reporter with a superb technique."

The Russo-Japanese War was undoubtedly the biggest single event in Ponting's career before his involvement in Scott's Antarctic expedition. The limitations of film and cameras of the period mean that the "war" photographs that come down to us cannot compare with the immediacy of those taken today—particularly as on the Japanese side the correspondents and photographers covering the war were not allowed anywhere near the action. However, the war does enable us to see Ponting in action through the eyes of a well-known correspondent colleague, Edwin Emerson, who wrote about Ponting in some detail in his book *Sunset*, published in 1905:

"[He is] the foremost war photographer in the Far East... Ponting is the man, whose exclusive photographs of Port Arthur, Mukden, Manchuria, Korea and the hostile war fleets in eastern waters were published broad-cast [widely] by Underwood and Underwood at the outset of the war. Ponting was the only one who had the gumption to travel through these regions on the eve of the outbreak of hostilities, photographing everything of warlike interest in spite of frequent arrests and danger of prolonged military imprisonment. When war broke out, his unsurpassed stereoscopic pictures of the most important places and men in the theatre of war, were in such demand scientific and general situation he was likely to encounter. One newspaper, the *West Australian*, described it as "the most perfect photographic equipment ever devised" while the *British Journal of Photography,* a little more circumspectly, referred in its June 1910 issue to an outfit "the like of which has probably never before been brought together." Teddy Evans, second-in-command to Scott, put it more boldly—"A colossal photographic outfit." The young geologist Frank Debenham, who in due course was to take over many of Ponting's photographic responsibilities during the Expedition's second year, and later still to head the Scott Polar Research Institute, early in the trip wrote perhaps a little enviously in his diary, published as *The Quiet Land: The Antarctic Diaries of Frank Debenham*: "[Ponting's] photos will be quite the most popular part of the Expedition for he has some perfectly marvellous instruments... One camera has a set of about 10 lenses and, as it has a large extension, he can do anything with it, from photomicrography [to] stereoscopic work."

The "NS" Newman-Sinclair
REFLEX KINE' CAMERA
No. 3 Model.

In the 1920s, Newman-Sinclair advertised their cine cameras by using a film strip of Ponting's footage from the Antarctic. Although the camera shown in the advertisement (above) was not identical to the cinematograph that Ponting took south with him, it would not have been dissimilar.

A lengthy stay in Antarctica, particularly before the era of wireless communication, was a challenging experience involving a sense of separation perhaps comparable to a lengthy mission aboard a submarine or spacecraft. Ponting's character had both negative and positive elements in facing such a trial. Unlike the gregarious Frank Hurley, he was basically a "loner" with a stiff and slightly fussy demeanor and without a marked sense of humor. Again unlike Hurley, he could never be regarded as a "team player"—and it is significant that he never attended any of the reunions held from 1925 onward by the survivors of the Scott Expedition. His background provided him with the manners that enabled him to fit easily into social gatherings, but for the most part he preferred to relentlessly pusue his chosen path without distractions from persons or events. He was set in his ways, so in the confined spaces both on the ship and in the hut much friction was created with his colleagues.

In the hut at Cape Evans, Ponting built an 8 x 6-foot (2.4 x 1.8-m) room (left) that served as the photographic darkroom and storage facility, as well as his sleeping area. The room was packed with equipment, clear up to its ceiling.

However, even if he was irked by the lack of physical activity during an Antarctic winter, dedication to his work provided some outlet. He built his own darkroom in the hut at Cape Evans and it became his personal area with a camp-bed for sleeping at night. This was done with the blessing of Scott, who wrote in his diary on April 13, 1911: "Such a palatial chamber [it was all of 8 feet long, 6 feet wide, and 8 feet high, or 2.4 by 1.8 by 2.4 m] for the development of negatives and prints can only be justified by the quality of the work produced in it, and is only justified in our case by the possession of such an artist as Ponting...." Scott commented on the neatness of everything, to which Ponting responded with typical candor: "...in matters photographic untidiness is abhorrent to me." It was there that he worked, and the processing of movie film in particular, while in some ways tedious, became a welcome way of consuming time during the long dark hours.

Ponting started his careful documentation of the expedition immediately upon joining the ship. Even during the gale on the voyage south, when there were fears that Terra Nova *would founder, he was hard at work.*

Ponting landscape which has an empty sky; if the Sun is included in the frame the bleed or glare effect is limited; and despite extreme contrast in a scene, usually there will be detail in both highlights and shadows. Ponting's claim to being called a "camera artist," rather than a photographer, may seem pretentious but it was justified by his results—which were matchless when printed in pastel tones of blue or green by the carbon process.

The men in charge of the animals—Meares of the dogs and Oates of the ponies—are the subject of this mid-winter photograph (left). Anyone visiting Cape Evans today can still feel much of the "atmosphere" that is apparent in many of Ponting's remarkable photographs taken in the hut or the stables.

Edward Wilson, chief of the expedition's science staff, was a talented artist but even he found benefit in Ponting's skills: "I remember how puzzled [Wilson] once was over one of his studies of Mt. Erebus," Ponting wrote. "He could not get the mountain to look high enough. My experience in photographing mountains showed me what was wrong. He had given the sketch too much sky. Taking a sheet of paper I placed it across the top of his drawing, cutting off three inches, and immediately the mountain rose. He was quite pleased, and thought it remarkable that he had not thought of such a simple expedient himself."

Ponting belonged to a school of photography which in many ways was not regarded as "artistic" by the aesthetic conventions of the time: he did not indulge in tricks or composites and sought straight, crisp effects with maximum depth of field and technically rigorous development. Yet in later years an art journal could write that "Mr Ponting's pictures possess qualities which are only looked for in the work of great painters" and a noted member of the Royal Academy, Sir John Lavery, after looking at a Ponting portfolio, was quoted as saying that, "If I were to have painted any of these scenes, I would not have altered either the composition or the lighting of any of them in any way whatsoever." This was testimony to Ponting's superlative ability to visualize, record, and reproduce a scene on paper with incomparable technical excellence.

Cecil Meares (above), photographed on his return with the support party for Scott's Southern Journey. Meares was in charge of the dogs until he left the expedition in 1912, at the same time as Ponting.

While landscape photography revealed Ponting as a complete master, other areas of his work were also of a high order. Hitherto his work as a portraitist has not been emphasized, but in fact some of his studies were superb: we see Meares showing the strain of exposure to the Antarctic elements, but looking with clear eyes and the gaze of an experienced, hardy traveler; there is Cherry-Garrard, returned from a challenging journey who looks at Ponting's camera with the somewhat less assured, although bright expression of a younger man; and there are several portraits of "Soldier" Oates, which somehow manage to reveal his complex character—resolute and to a degree inscrutable, but with a sardonic comment about to be brought forth. Images of everyday activities are less likely to aspire to the categories of high art, but they appear in the collection in great numbers—ranging from a festive dinner scene to excruciatingly cold outside work in the height of winter, and all characterized by clarity and maximum detail. "Atmosphere" is difficult to define but it is also there in many of the pictures—most impressively of all perhaps in the image of Oates and Meares contentedly smoking their pipes as they converse at the blubber stove, where we can almost feel the welcome warmth and smell the pungent aroma!

In his movie work—and in particular that devoted to portraying the fauna of Antarctica—Ponting revealed the same qualities inherent in his still work. A novice in motion pictures before Antarctica, he made sure that he received expert tuition before his departure and obviously practiced the techniques of the moving picture extensively before leaving. Much of his movie record was devoted to seals, penguins, and flying birds, and he demonstrated endless patience and persistence in achieving results that portrayed the life and death of the animals with a detail never before seen. As with still photography, the cinematographer's life was not always without incident, with attacks threatened from seals, skuas, and killer whales, thankfully without serious consequences.

It is natural to attempt a comparison between Ponting and Frank Hurley, as near contemporaries in the Antarctic. It needs to be emphasized that Ponting had significant advantages. He was far more experienced than Hurley—which was of great importance in dealing with the photographic procedures of the time—but even more important was the fact that while Ponting was allowed to do his photographic work to the exclusion of everything else, Hurley was a full member of Shackleton's 1914–17 *Endurance* expedition with activities thrust upon him that had nothing to do with photography. Thus Hurley was not infrequently forced to "snatch" pictures when he could, whereas Ponting could take time to strive for the perfect result. Moreover, the circumstances in which Hurley found himself as the *Endurance* saga unfolded were infinitely more stressful and demanding than anything Ponting faced—and extended further than being forced to destroy many hard-won plates. The record that Hurley made of the Shackleton expedition was a supreme achievement in the face of extremely adverse conditions. Moreover, as a member of that expedition from start to finish, Hurley's record is more complete than Ponting's, with images shot of events on Elephant Island, for example, having enormous impact.

Where Ponting's work is undoubtedly superior is where he was able to maximize the advantage of time—with the carefully visualized landscapes of high technical quality. While Ponting's skies are rarely empty, many of Hurley's are—showing almost certainly that he was not using one of the yellow or orange "screens" (filters) whose purpose was to darken the sky and render details of cloud. Ponting generally had a surer touch with composition and there is a suggestion in the extreme contrast of many of Hurley's pictures that Ponting was also more careful in processing film and plates—although once again this may partially result from the conditions under which Hurley was forced to work. Perhaps it would be appropriate to compare the relative merits of the two men (who subsequently evinced a high regard for each other's work) by a reference to mathematics: Ponting strove to get every picture 95 percent right as an absolute minimum, whatever the circumstances, while Hurley was content with 80 percent because it afforded more flexibility and speed. There is much to be said for both attitudes.

The comparison between the two contemporaries can be extended to place their—and particularly Ponting's—work in the context of photography in the Antarctic over the following century. There are now many research stations on the continent, and while by no means without danger, life there is infinitely more congenial for the scientists and others visiting and wintering there than for the early explorers. Photography—whether moving or still pictures—is virtually without exception in color.

So far as motion pictures are concerned, Ponting and Hurley must be regarded as trail blazers who were using equipment and film that have long been superseded by many systems up to our own time—where even now video is increasingly replacing film itself. But the situation as regards color still photography is by no means so clear cut. Color film (and digital camera color) is now of extremely high quality. While expeditions to Antarctica have long since declined in numbers, being replaced by long-term residencies at research stations, there are now many temporary residents taking color images for professional, technical, and personal reasons—and visits by professional photographers to take pictures for commercial photo libraries are by no means uncommon. Do their efforts supersede the black and white work of Herbert Ponting?

Paradoxically, the question is best answered in the work of a later professional photographer, the Swiss Emil Schulthess. He visited Antarctica during the International Geophysical Year (1957–58) and was accredited to the US Deep Freeze IV operation. A few years later he published an excellent collection of images in his *Antarctica: A Photographic Survey*. Schulthess shot both in black and white and in color. Much of the color work is as good as one would expect, with carefully chosen bright, colored clothing, and painted objects—such as tractors or helicopters—aiding the impact. But it is the black and white landscapes of icebergs and ice formations generally that impress infinitely more, and the quality of Schulthess's black and white work comes very close to rivaling that of Ponting. In the book, spreads of color are next to spreads of black and white and without exception the texture and tone of the latter are superior. Since the same skill was at work with both mediums, why was this? Almost certainly because, much of the time, Antarctica in broad daylight can be compared to the moon—it is an essentially monochromatic subject. In good conditions, the blue sky reflects off ice and water and the result often is an essay in a narrow range of blue tones, which can be rendered just as well in black and white and frequently with more impact.

Ponting and Hurley both took samples of one of the first practical color systems—Autochrome plates—to the Antarctic with them. The plates had a relatively short life, and color fidelity and quality were such that the plates could best be regarded as showing a promise for the future. But images which both photographers exposed of evening skies pointed to the one area where color photography in the Antarctic comes into its own. Ponting expressed disappointment at what he saw as his failure to obtain pictures of the aurora during the winter.

Over forty years later George Lowe, photographer on the British Trans-Antarctic Expedition, described in his book *Because It Is There* (published in 1959) the fall as "the answer to a colour photographer's prayer, with orange

This haunting photograph was taken from, rather than of, one of Ponting's favorite subjects, the Barne Glacier. In the distance toward the northwest, dark against the sunlight, lies Cape Barne.

Ponting was perhaps the first photographer truly to do justice to the natural wonders of the Antarctic, whether on land, or in the sea or—in this case—in the heavens. Although he was disappointed in general with his images of the aurora, one finds it difficult to believe that anyone would not be pleased with this particular photograph.

suns jerking and sizzling through strange mirages, golden snow beneath clouds of every conceivable colour—and the moon always in view, switching on like a lighthouse when dusk fell."

Atmospheric phenomena and their effect upon Earth are indeed a subject for the color camera. Ponting would have relished the use of present-day color film in Antarctica, but he would have used it where it was best suited. Almost certainly he would still find a major role for black and white photography; it is often regarded as the true art medium for photography, a view reinforced by its continued use by photographers today.

As soon as Ponting's still and motion-picture work was publicly presented, the response, from King George V downward, was uniformly favorable, as it had been in Antarctica when he showed expedition members some of the early processed images. Perhaps the most apt response was that of Frank Hurley himself, who arrived in London in November 1916 on his safe return from the *Endurance* expedition. He attended Ponting's lecture-film *With Captain Scott in the Antarctic* four times and wrote in his diary that the pictures "were the acme of photographic perfection… The show well deserves its world-wide merit, Ponting's manner and delivery being excellent." The two met and the Englishman gave the Australian a copy of *In Lotus-Land: Japan* inscribed—with a glance back to his years in the American West—"In tribute to a brother artist of the trail." Hurley was delighted by this and, despite his own undoubted achievements, recorded in *Once More Upon My Adventure* (published in 1966) that "Ponting was looked upon as being the leader in Antarctic photography." (Ponting repaid the compliment years later in 1930 when he wrote to a friend that "Hurley is a 'crackerjack' with the camera.")

Ponting himself expressed some regrets about his achievement. "I found the Antarctic a very disappointing region for photography," he wrote in *The Great White South*. "It was exasperating to find the weather so often thwart one when half-way to some goal—for a journey to a point even a few miles distant could not be undertaken lightly. My camera and kinematograph equipment weighed more than 200 lbs: and when visiting a point a few miles away it was wise to take camping kit and food for several days, lest a blizzard should descend upon us. Pulling a load of 400 lbs deadweight, two men could not maintain a greater pace than one mile per hour; and if the surface were bad their progress might be much slower … there was seldom a man available to help me with the photographic work, whereas in fine weather I could have used the services of two constantly. However, notwithstanding the many impediments with which Nature sought to baulk one, it was surprising how much could be accomplished by persistent effort, and by grasping every opportunity she gave whilst in more amicable humour."

Of course he accomplished much, but from a distance of almost a century it is possible to wish—such was the quality of his work—that he could have achieved even more. The drive for perfection had its drawbacks, and in explaining why he abandoned a plan to go with one of the sledging parties he wrote in *The Great White South* "The … journey would not have enabled me to take my own time over my work and photography in these regions is too important and difficult to be done in haste." Perhaps, but the historical record is the poorer for the fact that, despite the valiant efforts of such as Frank Debenham and Murray Levick, there was no Ponting to record the achievement and suffering of the various sledging parties—or to record for posterity, with his typical striking clarity, the faces of the Northern Party when they staggered toward the hut at Cape Evans in November 1912 after surviving an Antarctic winter in appalling circumstances—an achievement that went almost unnoticed in the tragic events that overwhelmed the expedition. If Ponting had gone with the southern parties the record might have been enriched by images of the five members of the Polar Party as they set out on their final journey—but of course Scott did not announce his choice for that party until the last moment, and even if Ponting had begun the journey it is most unlikely that, doubtless refusing to jettison most of his equipment, he would have managed to get that far. What must be readily acknowledged is that Hurley's record of the *Endurance* expedition is more complete (despite the enforced destruction of the negatives they could not carry with them) because of his presence throughout, save for the perilous trip to South Georgia.

A visual record is inevitably seen subsequently in the context of what it portrays, a factor that can powerfully enhance the impact of that record. Thus Hurley's achievement in Antarctica, quite apart from considerations of intrinsic merit, is seen against the backdrop of an expedition that can be fairly described as a brilliant failure—Shackleton got his companions home even if the expedition objectives were not fulfilled and *Endurance* did not survive. If the analogy is brought somewhat closer to the present on another frontier of exploration, we see Hurley's images in the same context as we look at images of the Apollo 13 mission to the Moon.

Ponting's images are on another plane—on that same one from which we look at pictures of the Apollo 1 fire at Cape Kennedy in 1967 or those of the Challenger and Columbia space shuttle disasters of 1986 and 2003. Whatever such images may actually show, we cannot separate them in our minds from our awareness of the tragic loss of life that took place off-camera.

That is why it is appropriate to end with the often-quoted words that Apsley Cherry-Garrard so elegantly and poignantly penned for his obituary of Ponting in the *Geographical Journal* in 1935:

"He came to do a job, did it and did it well. Here in these pictures is beauty linked to tragedy—one of the great tragedies—and the beauty is inconceivable for it is endless and runs to eternity."

GALLERY

AN ILLUSTRATED CATALOGUE

GALLERY

THE PHOTOGRAPHS TAKEN BY HERBERT PONTING ON SCOTT'S *TERRA NOVA* EXPEDITION, 1910–1913 IN THIS BOOK ARE DRAWN MOSTLY FROM THE ARCHIVES OF THE ROYAL GEOGRAPHICAL SOCIETY AND THE SCOTT POLAR RESEARCH INSTITUTE. THE FOLLOWING PAGES SHOW PHOTOGRAPHS FROM THE ROYAL GEOGRAPHICAL SOCIETY'S COLLECTION THAT ARE NOT SHOWN ELSEWHERE IN THE BOOK. AFTER EACH CAPTION THERE IS AN ARCHIVE NUMBER FOR REFERENCE.

The *Terra Nova*

Terra Nova sailing through the pack, December 11, 1910. *[A108/000751; SP4059]*

Terra Nova held up for the first time in the ice, December 11, 1910. *[A108/000753; SP4061]*

Terra Nova held up in the pack. Ice point in the foreground, December 13, 1910. *[A108/000761; SP4069]*

Terra Nova held up in the pack, December 13, 1910. *[A108/000763; SP4071]*

Terra Nova at ice foot. Cape Barne and glacier in background, January 15, 1911. *[A108/000868; SP4176]*

Terra Nova at ice foot off Hut Point, 1912. *[A108/001275; SP4583]*

Furling *Terra Nova's* upper topsail in the pack, December 1910. *[A108/001303; SP4611]*

Watering *Terra Nova* at Glacier Tongue, January 1911. *[A108/001318; SP4626]*

Terra Nova at ice foot (fine clouds) and Cape Barne, January 15, 1911. *[A108/001520; SP4828]*

Doctor Wilson and Lieutenant Pennell salting seal skins, December 27, 1910. *[A108/000775; SP4083]*

Lillie at the water bottle winch, January 1, 1911. *[A108/000794; SP4102]*

Nelson putting out the water bottle, January 1, 1911. *[A108/000795; SP4103]*

Lieutenant Rennick and the sounding machine, December 1910. *[A108/001291; SP4599]*

A fish is seen from the deck of *Terra Nova*, December 1910. *[A108/001295; SP4603]*

Bosun Cheetham and ice anchor, December 1910. *[A108/001298; SP4606]*

Mutton hanging in the shrouds on the deck of *Terra Nova,* December 1910. *[A108/001299; SP4607]*

Group on the deck of *Terra Nova,* 1910–1912. *[A108/001500; SP4808]*

Sailors making clothing on the deck of *Terra Nova,* 1910–1912. *[A108/001504; SP4812]*

Lieutenant Rennick at the sounding machine on board *Terra Nova,* 1910–1912. *[A108/001506; SP4814]*

McCarthy at the wheel. "Wolsey underwear," 1911. *[A108/001517; SP4825]*

F. Drake taking meteorological observations, 1910–1912. *[A108/001536; SP4844]*

Lieutenant Rennick cuts Lillie's hair (off New Zealand), 1910–1912. *[A108/001541; SP4849]*

Portrait of Jas. Denistoun on the deck of *Terra Nova,* 1910–1912. *[A108/001542; SP4850]*

Meares and dogs on the ice house, January 3, 1911. *[A108/000806; SP4114]*

Sunset off New Zealand, March 30, 1912. *[A108/001547; SP4855]*

Outdoor Life at Cape Evans

Lieutenant Evans washing at the pool, January 7, 1911. *[A108/000845; SP4153]*

Evans and Nelson making an ice cave, January 12, 1911. *[A108/000857; SP4165]*

Mt. Erebus from the ship; sledge and ballast in foreground, January 13, 1911. *[A108/000859; SP4167]*

Berg aground near Cape Evans. Boat coming off. *Terra Nova* aground, January 20, 1911. *[A108/000875; SP4183]*

Stacking patent fuel, January 23, 1911. *[A108/000880; SP4188]*

Interest in the trawl catch, January 24, 1911. *[A108/000881; SP4189]*

Wolsey underwear, February 7, 1911. *[A108/000885; SP4193]*

Mandelberg windproofs, February 7, 1911. *[A108/000886; SP4194]*

Sledging and a cup of Fry's, February 7, 1911. *[A108/000888; SP4196]*

Lieutenant Rennick with artificial horizon, February 9, 1911. *[A108/000894; SP4202]*

Ponting and Lashly with a squid found by Ponting at Cape Royds, February 16, 1911. *[A108/000918; SP4226]*

Nelson attaching townet to kite, March 15, 1911. *[A108/000959; SP4267]*

Nelson and Day landing the townet, March 15, 1911. *[A108/000960; SP4268]*

Doctor Wilson and Bowers reading the Ramp thermometer, June 7, 1911. *[A108/001021; SP4329]*

Day digging out the snow by motors, August 1, 1911. *[A108/001039; SP4347]*

C. S. Wright working at night with the transit, August 8, 1911. *[A108/001040; SP4348]*

Captain Scott, Simpson, Bowers, and Evans leaving, September 15, 1911. *[A108/001051; SP4359]*

Lieutenant Evans and one of the sledging theodolites (Barne Glacier in background), October 1911. *[A108/001091; SP4399]*

Lieutenant Evans surveying, October 1911. *[A108/001092; SP4400]*

Silt bands in Barne Glacier and Lieutenant Gran, October 1911. *[A108/001102; SP4410]*

Lieut. T. Gran turning on skis, October 1911. *[A108/001104; SP4412]*

Day and Hooper on return from the Barrier, December 21, 1911. *[A108/001183; SP4491]*

Nelson's igloo and sledge, December 24, 1911. *[A108/001188; SP4496]*

Nelson in igloo with water bottle (Nansen-Pettersson insulating), December 24, 1911. *[A108/001189; SP4497]*

Nelson with reversing thermometers, December 24, 1911. *[A108/001191; SP4499]*

Return of Atkinson's party, January 29, 1912. *[A108/001237; SP4545]*

Demetri and some of the dogs, 1912. *[A108/001259; SP4567]*

Lieutenant Pennell and prismatic compass in the pack, December 1910. *[A108/001289; SP4597]*

The whale boat off Cape Crozier, January 1911. *[A108/001309; SP4617]*

Mt. Erebus from the *Terra Nova* at the ice foot, January 1911. *[A108/001314; SP4622]*

Doctor Simpson entering the magnetic hut, March 1911. *[A108/001326; SP4634]*

Doctor Simpson inflating one of his balloons, April 7, 1911. *[A108/001330; SP4638]*

Doctor Wilson at the sunshine recorder, August 26, 1911. *[A108/001334; SP4642]*

C. H. Meares cutting up seal meat for the dogs, November 1911. *[A108/001356; SP4664]*

Heinz advertisement, January 9, 1911. *[A108/001421; SP4729]*

Hooper and Demetri with a seal, 1910–1912. *[A108/001475; SP4783]*

Watering the ship at Glacier Tongue, 1911. *[A108/001514; SP4822]*

Ernest Shackleton's hut, February 17, 1911. *[A108/000921; SP4229]*

The first warm sunny spring day (–15°F). Hut and Mt. Erebus, September 17, 1911. *[A108/001059; SP4367]*

Shackleton's hut and Mt. Erebus, November 27, 1911. *[A108/001151; SP4459]*

First appearance of the sun over the Barne Glacier. Hut in foreground, August 25, 1911. *[A108/001329; SP4637]*

First rays of sunshine on the hut and some fellows watching it, August 26, 1911. *[A108/001333; SP4641]*

Getting one of the motors on to the sea ice, October 1911. *[A108/001096; SP4404]*

Day and one of the motors. Mt. Erebus in the background, October 1911. *[A108/001097; SP4405]*

The motor party: Lieutenant Evans, Day, Lashly, and Hooper by one of the motors, October 1911. *[A108/001100; SP4408]*

Day and Lashly fixing up one of the motors for the start of the Southern Journey, November 1911. *[A108/001361; SP4669]*

Day, Nelson, and Lashly probing a crevasse on the Barne Glacier, February 21, 1911. *[A108/000926; SP4234]*

Demetri and his dog team, 1912. *[A108/001260; SP4568]*

Captain Scott, Doctor Simpson, Lieutenant Bowers, and Evans leaving the hut for the west. Going on to the sea ice, September 15, 1911. *[A108/001337; SP4645]*

Indoor Life at Cape Evans

Nelson, Day, and Lashly in Shackleton's hut, February 17, 1911. *[A108/000922; SP4230]*

Interior of darkroom, March 24, 1911. *[A108/000968; SP4276]*

Taylor, Debenham, and Gran in cubicle, May 18, 1911. *[A108/001001; SP4309]*

Doctor Wilson working up a sketch, May 19, 1911. *[A108/001003; SP4311]*

A. C. Cherry-Garrard and his typewriter, June 8, 1911. *[A108/001024; SP4332]*

Midwinter Day tree, June 22, 1911. *[A108/001027; SP4336]*

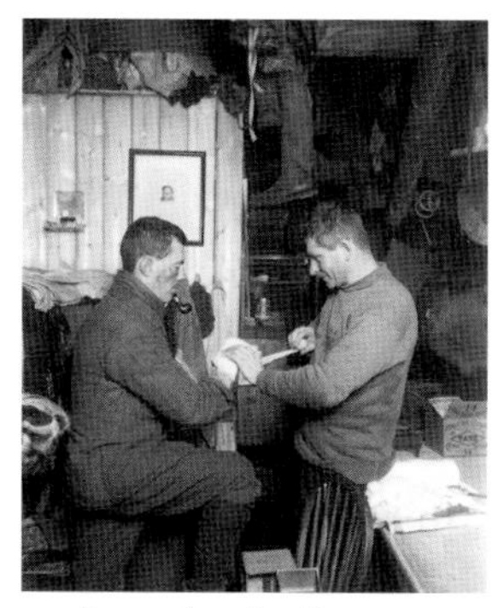

Seaman Evans dressing Doctor Atkinson's frostbitten hand, July 6, 1911. *[A108/001032; SP4340]*

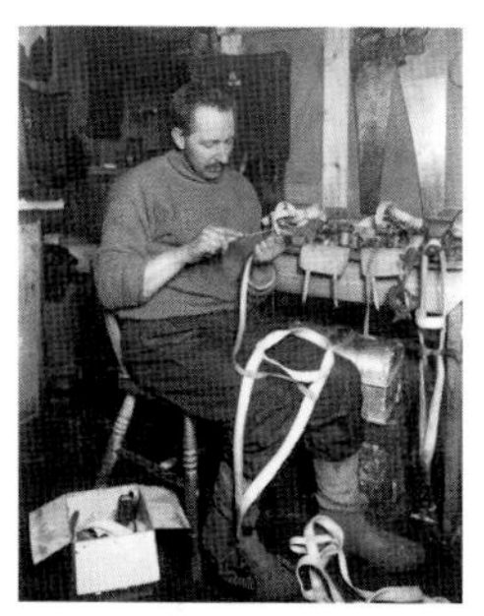

C. H. Meares making a dog harness, July 19, 1911. *[A108/001036; SP4344]*

Evans, Ford, and Crean putting a sledge together, August 30, 1911. *[A108/001044; SP4352]*

C. H. Meares and Demetri by the blubber stove in the *Discovery* hut, November 3, 1911. *[A108/001109; SP4417]*

Doctor Simpson in his lab, December 21, 1911. *[A108/001182; SP4490]*

Doctor Simpson at work in the magnetic hut, January 5, 1912. *[A108/001203; SP4511]*

Doctor Simpson at work in the magnetic hut, January 1912. *[A108/001204; SP4512]*

Doctor Simpson at the cloud chart, January 1912. *[A108/001205; SP4513]*

Packing sugar for sledging rations, January 1912. *[A108/001230; SP4538]*

The cook Clissold making pies, January 1912. *[A108/001239; SP4547]*

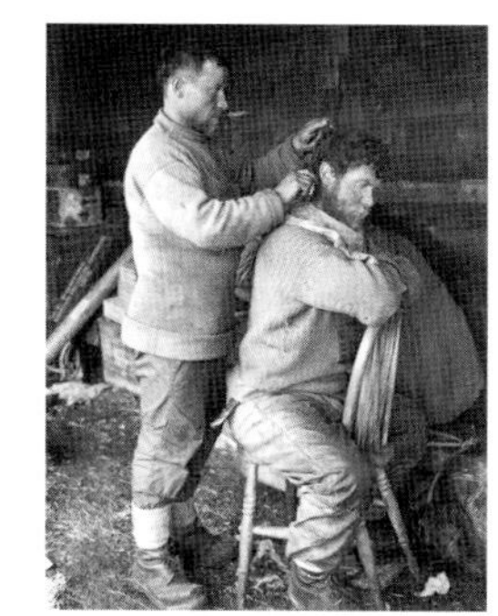

Hair cutting: Anton and P. Keohane, January 1912. *[A108/001240; SP4548]*

Dyne's anemometer in Simpson's lab registering 50 miles (80 km) an hour, 1912. *[A108/001253; SP4561]*

Portraits

Some of the *Terra Nova* crew on the fo'c'sle, December 28, 1910. *[A108/000776; SP4084]*

F. E. Debenham, April 13, 1911. *[A108/000983; SP4291]*

Lieutenant Bowers, April 13, 1911. *[A108/000984; SP4292]*

C. H. Meares and dog Osman, August 28, 1911. *[A108/001042; SP4350]*

A. C. Cherry-Garrard, November 1911. *[A108/001344; SP4652]*

Captain Scott at the ice crack, October 8, 1911. *[A108/001067; SP4375]*

Clissold on the Matterhorn Berg, October 8, 1911. *[A108/001075; SP4382]*

Ponting on the Matterhorn Berg, October 8, 1911. *[A108/001076; SP4384]*

Lieutenant Gran at Glacier Tongue, January 1911. *[A108/001512; SP4820]*

Full length portrait of Doctor Wilson standing at the door of the hut, October 1911. *[A108/001106; SP4414]*

Captain Oates, January 1912. *[A108/001242; SP4550]*

Doctor Atkinson, October 1911. *[A108/001108; SP4416]*

Lieutenant Evans by the motor, November 1911. *[A108/001336; SP4644]*

C. S. Wright, November 1911. *[A108/001340; SP4648]*

Seaman Crean, November 1911. *[A108/001345; SP4653]*

Seaman Keohane, November 1911. *[A108/001346; SP4654]*

Seaman Forde, November 1911. *[A108/001347; SP4655]*

Petty Officer Evans, November 1911. *[A108/001352; SP4660]*

Mechanic Lashly, November 1911. *[A108/001354; SP4662]*

B. C. Day by the motor, November 1911. *[A108/001343; SP4651]*

Antarctic Animals

Skua gull and chick, January 6, 1911. *[A108/000834; SP4142]*

Skua gull feeding chick, January 6, 1911. *[A108/000837; SP4145]*

Skua's nest and eggs, January 1912. *[A108/001210; SP4518]*

Skua settling on eggs, January 1912. *[A108/001215; SP4523]*

Young (three-day) chicks in nest, January 1912. *[A108/001223; SP4531]*

Sooty albatross on the wing, 1910–1912. *[A108/001533; SP4841]*

Weddell seal diving off the ice. Cape Evans, March 15, 1911. *[A108/000965; SP4273]*

Young Weddell seal, November 9, 1911. *[A108/001128; SP4436]*

Weddell seal and calf at Razorback, November 9, 1911. *[A108/0001129; SP4437]*

Seal coming up to breathe, November 19, 1911. *[A108/001138; SP4446]*

Seal with calf, November 19, 1911. *[A108/001142; SP4450]*

Seals at Razorback, November 19, 1911. *[A108/001145; SP4453]*

Killer whales off Barne Glacier, 1912. *[A108/001262; SP4570]*

Penguins and an iceberg, January 7, 1911. *[A108/000839; SP4147]*

Mt. Erebus from ice foot with penguins in foreground, January 13, 1911. *[A108/000861; SP4169]*

Rennick and Drake making friendly advances to Adélie penguins, February 9, 1911. *[A108/000895; SP4203]*

Rennick and a friendly Adélie penguin, February 9, 1911. *[A108/000898; SP4206]*

A corner of the penguinery at Cape Royds, February 13, 1911. *[A108/000907; SP4215]*

Penguins and a berg at Cape Royds, February 13, 1911. *[A108/000910; SP4218]*

On the penguinery, Cape Royds, November 26, 1911. *[A108/001157; SP4465]*

Adélie penguins love-making, December 8, 1911. *[A108/001171; SP4479]*

Herbert Ponting on the penguinery. Cape Royds, November 1911. *[A108/001365; SP4673]*

Angry penguin attacking Herbert Ponting. Cape Royds, November 1911. *[A108/001369; SP4677]*

Ecstatic Adélie penguin, November 1911. *[A108/001377; SP4685]*

Adélie penguin: attitude study, November 1911. *[A108/001378; SP4686]*

Adélie penguin: attitude study, November 1911. *[A108/001395; SP4703]*

Clissold and an Emperor penguin, 1910–1912. *[A108/001488; SP4796]*

Some of the ponies on *Terra Nova*, 1910–1912. *[A108/000786; SP4094]*

Captain Oates and pony Snippets, October 1911. *[A108/001085; SP4393]*

Lieutenant Bowers and pony Victor, October 1911. *[A108/001086; SP4394]*

Seaman Crean and pony Bones, October 1911. *[A108/001087; SP4395]*

Seaman Keohane and pony Jimmy Pig, October 1911. *[A108/001089; SP4397]*

C. S. Wright and pony Chinaman, 1910–1912. *[A108/001425; SP4733]*

Husky Hohol, 1910–1912. *[A108/001427; SP4735]*

Husky Lappy, 1910–1912. *[A108/001428; SP4736]*

Husky Wolk, 1910–1912. *[A108/001431; SP4739]*

Husky Julik, 1910–1912. *[A108/001439; SP4747]*

Husky Brodiaga, 1910–1912. *[A108/001440; SP4748]*

Husky Osman, 1910–1912. *[A108/001467; SP4775]*

Husky Koomagai, 1910–1912. *[A108/001470; SP4778]*

Landscapes

A large tabular berg, December 9, 1910. *[A108/000749; SP4057]*

Detail of the pack, December 11, 1910. *[A108/000755; SP4063]*

Telephoto of tilted barrier berg, December 18, 1910. *[A108/000764; SP4072]*

Telephoto. Large berg in pack, December 20, 1910. *[A108/000767; SP4075]*

Young pancake ice forming at West Beach. Mt. Erebus in background, March 9, 1911. *[A108/000956; SP4264]*

Lead opening and shadow of bowsprit, December 28, 1910. *[A108/000778; SP4086]*

In the pack. Sky reflection, December 28, 1910. *[A108/000781; SP4089]*

Ross Sea. Open water and clouds, about 11:00 a.m., January 2, 1911. *[A108/000803; SP4111]*

End of the Barrier, January 3, 1911. *[A108/000812; SP4120]*

Glacier breaking away off the Cape Crozier penguin rookery, January 3, 1911. *[A108/000814; SP4122]*

Mt. Erebus at 7:00 p.m., January 3, 1911. *[A108/000818; SP4126]*

Mt. Erebus at 1:15 a.m., January 4, 1911. *[A108/000823; SP4131]*

Mt. Erebus at 1:30 a.m., January 4, 1911. *[A108/000823; SP4132]*

An Antarctic cascade near the house, January 7, 1911. *[A108/000842; SP4150]*

Skua gulls on the floe, January 9, 1911. *[A108/000852; SP4160]*

Mt. Erebus from the ship, sledges on ice, and light effect on the snow, January 13, 1911. *[A108/000858; SP4166]*

Mt. Erebus's summit, January 13, 1911. *[A108/000863; SP4171]*

Cloud effect at Cape Royds and berg, February 15, 1911. *[A108/000913; SP4221]*

Cape Royds looking north, February 15, 1911. *[A108/000914; SP4222]*

Cape Royds looking south, February 15, 1911. *[A108/000915; SP4223]*

Mt. Erebus from West Beach at 5:00 p.m., March 7, 1911. *[A108/000942; SP4250]*

Bergs and floe off Cape Evans, March 7, 1911. *[A108/000945; SP4253]*

North Beach, camp, and Mt. Erebus from the west, March 7, 1911. *[A108/000946; SP4254]*

Young pancake ice forming at West Beach. Mt. Erebus in background, March 9, 1911. *[A108/000955; SP4263]*

Pancake ice forming on sea, March 9, 1911. *[A108/000957; SP4265]*

North Bay and camp from the east, March 16, 1911. *[A108/000966; SP4274]*

Sun rising behind Mt. Erebus at 9:30 a.m., March 29, 1911. *[A108/000976; SP4284]*

Mirage of Cape Barne and glacier, March 16, 1911. *[A108/000979; SP4287]*

Land's End and adjoining glacier, April 28, 1911. *[A108/000992; SP4300]*

Entrance to Land's End Glacier. Captain Scott, April 28, 1911. *[A108/000995; SP4303]*

Looking to Tent Island from one of the caves. Captain Scott and Wright, April 28, 1911. *[A108/000997; SP4305]*

Telephoto of smoke from Mt. Erebus 10:00 a.m., September 9, 1911. *[A108/001048; SP4356]*

The point of the Barne Glacier (where it turns round to the Bay before Cape Barne), September 18, 1911. *[A108/001061; SP4369]*

Mt. Erebus across the ice crack, October 8, 1911. *[A108/001070; SP4378]*

The face of the Matterhorn Berg (just before Clissold fell), October 8, 1911. *[A108/001074; SP4383]*

Discovery hut and the gap, November 4, 1911. *[A108/001110; SP4418]*

The Vince Cross at Hut Point and Mt. Discovery in the distance (and nice sky effect), November 4, 1911. *[A108/001111; SP4419]*

Castle Rock, November 5, 1911. *[A108/001118; SP4426]*

Mt. Erebus and berg as we floated off. 4:45 p.m., January 20, 1911. *[A108/000874; SP4182]*

Mt. Erebus and Back Door Bay, Cape Royds, November 27, 1911. *[A108/001152; SP4460]*

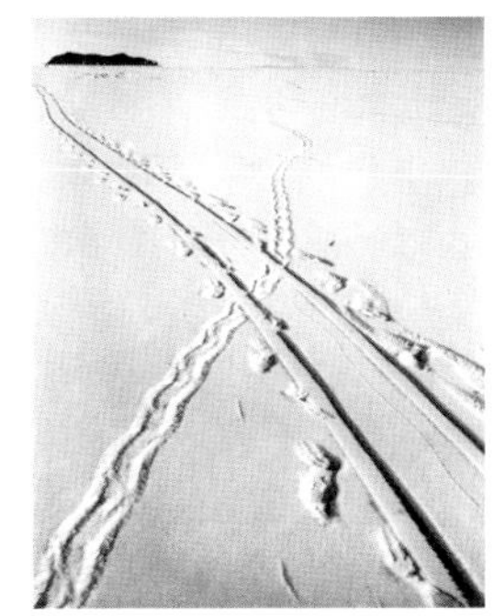

Adélie penguin track and sledge track crossing, December 8, 1911. *[A108/001170; SP4478]*

Cumulus cloud over the Barne Glacier, December 2, 1911. *[A108/001173; SP4481]*

Approaching snow storm, about 3:00 p.m., December 18, 1911. *[A108/001174; SP4482]*

Barne Glacier and cloud effect, December 1911. *[A108/001175; SP4483]*

Beautiful cirrus clouds over Barne Glacier, December 19, 1911. *[A108/001181; SP4489]*

Telephoto of Church Berg, seals, and Western Mountains from Vane Hill, December 27, 1911. *[A108/001196; SP4504]*

Church Berg and seals, December 29, 1911. *[A108/001197; SP4505]*

Hut and Western Mountains, January 1912. *[A108/001226; SP4534]*

Turk's Head from Glacier Front, January 1912. *[A108/001227; SP4535]*

Front of Turk's Head Glacier looking north, January 1912. *[A108/001229; SP4537]*

Ice breaking up off Cape Evans, January 30, 1912. *[A108/001233; SP4541]*

Iridescent clouds over Barne Glacier, 1912. *[A108/001254; SP4562]*

Cloud effect over Barne Glacier, 1912. *[A108/001255; SP4563]*

Hut Point and Observation Hill from *Terra Nova*, March 4, 1912. *[A108/001274; SP4582]*

Curious clouds and earth shadow on Mt. Erebus, 9:45 a.m., March 26, 1911. *[A108/001321; SP4629]*

The gallery shows examples of the photographs taken by Herbert Ponting on Scott's *Terra Nova* Expedition, 1910–1913. In many cases, the archive at the Royal Geographical Society contains several similar pictures within each category. In addition to those illustrated on pages 226–235, others on the same subjects are listed below.

The *Terra Nova*

Entering the pack. Fo'c'sle of the *Terra Nova*, December 9, 1910. *[A108/000746; SP4054]*

The *Terra Nova* held up for the first time in the ice, December 11, 1910. *[A108/000753; SP4061]*

The *Terra Nova* held up in the pack, December 13, 1910. *[A108/000757; SP4065]*

The *Terra Nova* held up in the pack, December 13, 1910. *[A108/000758; SP4067]*

The *Terra Nova* held up in the pack. Ice point in the foreground, December 13, 1910. *[A108/000761; SP4069]*

The *Terra Nova* held up in the pack. Ice point in the foreground, December 13, 1910. *[A108/000762; SP4070]*

The *Terra Nova* held up in the pack, December 13, 1910. *[A108/000763; SP4071]*

The prow of the *Terra Nova* opening the pack, December 19, 1910. *[A108/000765; SP4073]*

Surgeon Levick skinning a penguin on the *Terra Nova*, 1910–1912. *[A108/000784; SP4092]*

Lillie getting a townet out, January 1, 1911. *[A108/000793; SP4101]*

Nelson sending down the water bottle, January 1, 1911. *[A108/000796; SP4104]*

Nelson and Lillie with water bottle closed, January 1, 1911. *[A108/000797; SP4105]*

Nelson and Lillie taking sample from bottle, January 1, 1911. *[A108/000798; SP4106]*

Ross Sea. Cloud effect at 7:00 p.m. Ship's rail in foreground, January 2, 1911. *[A108/000804; SP4112]*

The *Terra Nova* and a berg at ice foot, January 16, 1911. *[A108/000871; SP4179]*

Lillie and Levick examining the trawl catch, January 24, 1911. *[A108/000882; SP4190]*

The *Terra Nova* lying off Barne Glacier, February 8, 1911. *[A108/000890; SP4198]*

The *Terra Nova* lying off the shore from the hut, February 8, 1911. *[A108/000891; SP4199]*

The last boat for the ship, February 9, 1911. *[A108/000900; SP4208]*

Lillie with a large glass sponge, 1912. *[A108/001272; SP4580]*

Terra Nova at ice foot off Hut Point, 1912. *[A108/001276; SP4584]*

Doctor Levick skinning a penguin on the *Terra Nova*, December 1910. *[A108/001290; SP4598]*

Doctor Levick skinning a penguin on the *Terra Nova*, December 1910. *[A108/001292; SP4600]*

The *Terra Nova* at the ice foot off Cape Evans, January 1911. *[A108/001307; SP4615]*

The *Terra Nova* at Glacier Tongue, January 1911. *[A108/001315; SP4623]*

Captain Scott and Lieutenant Evans on the deck of the *Terra Nova*, December 1910. *[A108/001499; SP4807]*

On *Terra Nova* "at the pumps," December 1910. *[A108/001502; SP4810]*

F. Drake reading the compass on the deck of the *Terra Nova*, 1910–1912. *[A108/001505; SP4813]*

F. Drake taking the temperature of the sea on board *Terra Nova*, 1910–1912. *[A108/001507; SP4815]*

Lieutenant Evans entering the crow's nest of *Terra Nova*, 1910–1912. *[A108/001522; SP4830]*

F. Drake taking meteorological observations, 1910–1912. *[A108/001535; SP4843]*

F. Drake on the deck of the *Terra Nova*, 1910–1912. *[A108/001537; SP4845]*

Mr. Williams at the sounding engine on the deck of the *Terra Nova*, 1910–1912. *[A108/001538; SP4846]*

Herbert Ponting cinematographing a heavy gale from the bridge of the *Terra Nova*, 1910–1912. *[A108/001540; SP4848]*

Portrait of Lieutenant Rennick on the deck of *Terra Nova* (off New Zealand), 1910–1912. *[A108/001543; SP4851]*

Group on the fo'c'sle off New Zealand (deck of *Terra Nova*), 1910–1912. *[A108/001544; SP4852]*

Portrait of Lieutenant Rennick on the deck of *Terra Nova* (off New Zealand), 1910–1912. *[A108/001545; SP4853]*

Group on the fo'c'sle off New Zealand, 1910–1912. *[A108/001546; SP4854]*

Outdoor Life at Cape Evans

Doctor Wilson skinning a seal on the ice, January 7, 1911. *[A108/000846; SP4154]*

Drake, a member of the crew, pulls sledge carrying blocks of ice to melt for drinking water, January 10, 1911. *[A108/000856; SP4164]*

Mather and sledge of ballast, January 14, 1911. *[A108/000864; SP4172]*

Piling stores near hut. Colman's flour, January 23, 1911. *[A108/000879; SP4187]*

Rennick and Drake making friendly advances to Adélie penguins, February 9, 1911. *[A108/000896; SP4204]*

Rennick and Drake making friendly advances to Adélie penguins, February 9, 1911. *[A108/000897; SP4205]*

The whaler leaving for the *Terra Nova*, February 9, 1911. *[A108/000899; SP4207]*

Left behind in Victoria Land, February 9, 1911. *[A108/000901; SP4209]*

Packing a sledge at the top of the moraine for a trip to Shackleton's, February 11, 1911. *[A108/000903; SP4211]*

Packing a sledge at the top of the moraine for a trip to Shackelton's, February 11, 1911. *[A108/000904; SP4212]*

Day, Nelson, and Lashly staking out the Barne Glacier, February 11, 1911. *[A108/000905; SP4213]*

Cape Royds from the glacier between Cape Barne and Royds, February 11, 1911. *[A108/000906; SP4214]*

Day and Nelson on Clear Lake. Cape Royds, February 15, 1911. *[A108/000916; SP4224]*

Day and Nelson on Clear Lake. Cape Royds, February 15, 1911. *[A108/000917; SP4225]*

Ernest Shackleton's hut, February 17, 1911. *[A108/000921; SP4229]*

Day, Nelson, Lashly, and sledge on Barne Glacier, February 21, 1911. *[A108/000924; SP4232]*

Day, Nelson, and Lashly among crevasses on Barne Glacier, February 21, 1911. *[A108/000927; SP4235]*

Entrance to cave in Land's End Glacier with Wright, April 28, 1911. *[A108/000994; SP4302]*

Looking to Tent Island from one of the caves. Captain Scott and Wright, April 28, 1911. *[A108/000998; SP4306]*

Doctor Atkinson and Clissold taking in the fish trap (–40°F), May 28, 1911. *[A108/001012; SP4320]*

Doctor Wilson, Cherry-Garrard, and Forde with a sea leopard on a sledge, May 28, 1911. *[A108/001015; SP4323]*

Oates and Meares on skis, June 4, 1911. *[A108/001017; SP4325]*

Ponting cutting a hole in the ice for lowering the fish trap, June 26, 1911. *[A108/001029; SP4337]*

F. Debenham and weathered Kenyte, September 9, 1911. *[A108/001050; SP4358]*

A blizzard beginning on Mt. Erebus, October 1, 1911. *[A108/001062; SP4370]*

Clissold and his dog sledge, October 1, 1911. *[A108/001063; SP4371]*

Day and the motor garage, October 5, 1911. *[A108/001064; SP4372]*

Day and the motor garage, October 5, 1911. *[A108/001065; SP4373]*

Harnessing Michael to the sledge, October 1911. *[A108/001090; SP4398]*

A motor leaving the winter "garage," October 1911. *[A108/001094; SP4402]*

Getting one of the motors on to the sea ice, October 1911. *[A108/001095; SP4403]*

Day and one of the motors, October 1911. *[A108/001098; SP4406]*

Loaded sledges for one of the motors on the sea ice, October 1911. *[A108/001099; SP4407]*

Lieut. T. Gran on skis, October 1911. *[A108/001103; SP4411]*

Demetri's dogs (with Demetri) ready to start south, November 5, 1911. *[A108/001115; SP4423]*

C. H. Meares and Demetri with their dog teams ready to start south, November 5, 1911. *[A108/001116; SP4424]*

C. H. Meares and Demetri with their dog teams southward bound from Hut Point, November 5, 1911. *[A108/001117; SP4425]*

Ponting and Nelson camped by the penguinery, Cape Royds, November 27, 1911. *[A108/001153; SP4461]*

Herbert Ponting and photo go-cart with dogs, Mass Johnson and Lassie, December 24, 1911. *[A108/001186; SP4494]*

Nelson letting down the water bottle, December 24, 1911. *[A108/001190; SP4498]*

Nelson with thermometers reversed, December 24, 1911. *[A108/001192; SP4500]*

Return of Atkinson's party, January 29, 1912. *[A108/001237; SP4545]*

Return of Atkinson's party, January 29, 1912. *[A108/001238; SP4546]*

Doctor Atkinson's dog team landing stores from ship, 1912. *[A108/001258; SP4566]*

A party landing stores from the ship, 1912. *[A108/001261; SP4569]*

Boat going to the hut from the ship 3:00 a.m., March 4, 1912. *[A108/001278; SP4586]*

Nelson and Priestley making a hole in a floe, December 1910. *[A108/001287; SP4595]*

Doctor Wilson loading the whale gun, December 1910. *[A108/001296; SP4604]*

Captain Oates and Seaman Abbott picketing ponies, January 1911. *[A108/001310; SP4618]*

Watering the *Terra Nova* at Glacier Tongue, January 1911. *[A108/001316; SP4624]*

Doctor Simpson leaving the magnetograph ice cave, March 1911. *[A108/001325; SP4633]*

Doctor Simpson taking observations on Vane Hill; B. Day and balloon theodolite, March 16, 1911. *[A108/001328; SP4636]*

Doctor Wilson watching the record receiving the Sun's first rays of the season, August 26, 1911. *[A108/001332; SP4640]*

Captain Scott, Doctor Simpson, Lieutenant Bowers, and Evans leaving the hut for the west, September 15, 1911. *[A108/001339; SP4647]*

Wright and Bowers packing sledges for the Southern Journey, November 1911. *[A108/001358; SP4666]*

Ponting making a hole in the ice, June 26, 1911. *[A108/001519; SP4827]*

Indoor Life at Cape Evans

Interior of darkroom, March 24, 1911. *[A108/000969; SP4277]*

Interior of darkroom: the sink, March 24, 1911. *[A108/000970; SP4278]*

Nelson's and Day's bunks, March 25, 1911. *[A108/000971; SP4279]*

Ponting's bed in darkroom, March 25, 1911. *[A108/000972; SP4280]*

Simpson's laboratory, March 31, 1911. *[A108/000978; SP4286]*

Evans and Crean mending sleeping bags, May 16, 1911. *[A108/000999; SP4307]*

Doctor Wilson working up a sketch, May 18, 1911. *[A108/001002; SP4310]*

Taylor and Debenham in cubicle, May 19, 1911. *[A108/001004; SP4312]*

Anton cooking mashes in the stable, May 23, 1911. *[A108/001007; SP4315]*

Meares and Oates at the blubber stove, May 26, 1911. *[A108/001011; SP4319]*

A winter work group, June 6, 1911. *[A108/001020; SP4328]*

Midwinter work group, June 8, 1911. *[A108/001023; SP4331]*

Midwinter Day Dinner, June 22, 1911. *[A108/001026; SP4334]*

The gas plant, December 20, 1911. *[A108/001179; SP4487]*

The gas plant, December 20, 1911. *[A108/001180; SP4488]*

Portraits

Captain Scott, just before leaving for the Southern Journey, January 26, 1911. *[A108/000883; SP4191]*

Evans and Crean, April 13, 1911. *[A108/000989; SP4297]*

Dr. E. A. Wilson, April 21, 1911. *[A108/000991; SP4299]*

Doctor Atkinson's frostbitten hand, July 5, 1911. *[A108/001031; SP4339]*

Captain Oates at the stable door, August 30, 1911. *[A108/001046; SP4353]*

Captain Scott at the ice crack, October 8, 1911. *[A108/001068; SP4376]*

Portrait of Lieutenant Bowers, October 11, 1911. *[A108/001079; SP4387]*

Captain Scott on skis, October 1911. *[A108/001093; SP4401]*

Western Geological Party: F. Debenham, T. G. Taylor, T. Gran, and Forde, 1912. *[A108/001269; SP4577]*

Western Geological Party: F. Debenham, T. G. Taylor, T. Gran, and Forde, 1912. *[A108/001270; SP4578]*

Group of officers of *Terra Nova*, 1912. *[A108/001282; SP4590]*

C. H. Meares and dog Osman, August 26, 1911. *[A108/001335; SP4643]*

C. S. Wright, November 1911. *[A108/001341; SP4649]*

B. C. Day by the motor, November 1911. *[A108/001342; SP4650]*

Seaman Forde, November 1911. *[A108/001348; SP4656]*

Petty Officer Evans, November 1911. *[A108/001349; SP4657]*

Petty Officer Evans, November 1911. *[A108/001350; SP4658]*

Petty Officer Evans, November 1911. *[A108/001351; SP4659]*

Mechanic Lashly, November 1911. *[A108/001353; SP4661]*

Steward Hooper, November 1911. *[A108/001355; SP4663]*

Lieutenant Evans at Glacier Tongue, January 1911. *[A108/001510; SP4818]*

Lieutenant Evans at Glacier Tongue, January 1911. *[A108/001511; SP4819]*

Lieutenant Bowers at Glacier Tongue, January 1911. *[A108/001513; SP4821]*

Emperor penguin's eggs, January 1912. *[A108/001244; SP4552]*

A Notothenia, 1912. *[A108/001245; SP4553]*

Sledging rations for one man for one day, 1912. *[A108/001246; SP4554]*

Finnesko (boots), 1912. *[A108/001247; SP4555]*

Ski shoes for finnesko (boots), 1912. *[A108/001248; SP4556]*

Ski adaptation for finnesko (boots), 1912. *[A108/001249; SP4557]*

Crampons for finnesko (boots), 1912. *[A108/001250; SP4558]*

Antarctic Animals

Penguins on the floe, December 24, 1910. *[A108/000773; SP4081]*

Penguins resting, January 7, 1911. *[A108/000840; SP4148]*

Penguins resting, January 7, 1911. *[A108/000841; SP4149]*

Sky effect (midnight Sun) and penguins at ice edge, January 13, 1911. *[A108/000862; SP4170]*

Adélie penguins "porpoising," January 15, 1911. *[A108/000866; SP4174]*

Adélie penguins "porpoising," January 15, 1911. *[A108/000867; SP4175]*

Penguins making for the water, January 16, 1911. *[A108/000870; SP4178]*

Penguins and a berg at Cape Royds, February 13, 1911. *[A108/000908; SP4216]*

Penguins and a berg at Cape Royds, February 13, 1911. *[A108/000909; SP4217]*

Group of young penguins. Cape Royds, February 14, 1911. *[A108/000911; SP4219]*

Moulting penguin, February 18, 1911. *[A108/000923; SP4231]*

On the penguinery. Cape Royds, November 26, 1911. *[A108/001155; SP4463]*

On the penguinery. Cape Royds, November 26, 1911. *[A108/001156; SP4464]*

On the penguinery. Cape Royds, November 26, 1911. *[A108/001157; SP4465]*

The penguinery after a blizzard. Cape Royds, December 8, 1911. *[A108/001158; SP4466]*

The penguinery after a blizzard. Cape Royds, December 8, 1911. *[A108/001159; SP4467]*

The penguinery after a blizzard. Cape Royds, December 8, 1911. *[A108/001160; SP4468]*

Penguins snowed up, December 8, 1911. *[A108/001161; SP4469]*

On the penguinery after a blizzard, December 8, 1911. *[A108/001162; SP4470]*

Sitting penguin snowed up, only head showing, December 8, 1911. *[A108/001163; SP4471]*

Sitting penguin snowed up, only head showing, December 8, 1911. *[A108/001164; SP4472]*

Sitting penguin snowed up, December 8, 1911. *[A108/001165; SP4473]*

Sitting penguin snowed up, December 8, 1911. *[A108/001166; SP4474]*

Sitting penguin snowed up, only head and tail showing, December 8, 1911. *[A108/001167; SP4475]*

Penguin spread-eagled, December 8, 1911. *[A108/001168; SP4476]*

The penguinery after the blizzard with Mt. Erebus behind, December 8, 1911. *[A108/001169; SP4477]*

Adélie penguins: a heated argument, December 8, 1911. *[A108/001172; SP4480]*

E. W. Nelson on the penguinery. Cape Royds, November 1911. *[A108/001364; SP4672]*

Herbert Ponting stroking a penguin on a nest. Cape Royds, November 1911. *[A108/001366; SP4674]*

Herbert Ponting stroking a penguin on a nest. Cape Royds, November 1911. *[A108/001367; SP4675]*

Angry penguin attacking Herbert Ponting, November 1911. *[A108/001368; SP4676]*

Adélie's snug nest amid rocks, November 1911. *[A108/001370; SP4678]*

Adélie's snug nest amid rocks, November 1911. *[A108/001371; SP4679]*

Some Adélie penguin nests are mounds of stones, November 1911. *[A108/001372; SP4680]*

"Ecstatic" Adélie penguin on nest, November 1911. *[A108/001373; SP4681]*

Other Adélie nests have no stones at all, November 1911. *[A108/001374; SP4682]*

"Ecstatic" Adélie penguin, November 1911. *[A108/001375; SP4683]*

"Ecstatic" Adélie penguin with eggs, November 1911. *[A108/001376; SP4684]*

Adélie penguin: attitude study, November 1911. *[A108/001379; SP4687]*

Adélie penguin: attitude study, November 1911. *[A108/001380; SP4688]*

Adelie penguin: attitude study, November 1911. *[A108/001381; SP4689]*

Adélie penguin: attitude study, November 1911. *[A108/001382; SP4690]*

Adélie penguin: attitude study, November 1911. *[A108/001383; SP4691]*

Adélie penguin: attitude study, November 1911. *[A108/001384; SP4692]*

Adélie penguin: attitude study, November 1911. *[A108/001385; SP4693]*

Adélie penguin: attitude study, November 1911. *[A108/001386; SP4694]*

Adélie penguin: attitude study, November 1911. *[A108/001387; SP4695]*

Adélie penguin: attitude study, November 1911. *[A108/001388; SP4696]*

Adelie penguin: attitude study, November 1911. *[A108/001389; SP4697]*

Adélie penguin: attitude study, November 1911. *[A108/001390; SP4698]*

Adélie penguin: attitude study, November 1911. *[A108/001391; SP4699]*

Adélie penguin: attitude study, November 1911. *[A108/001392; SP4700]*

Adélie penguin: attitude study, November 1911. *[A108/001393; SP4701]*

Adélie penguin: attitude study, November 1911. *[A108/001394; SP4702]*

Adélie penguin: attitude study, November 1911. *[A108/001396; SP4704]*

Adélie penguin about to turn eggs, November 1911. *[A108/001397; SP4705]*

Adélie penguin turning eggs, November 1911. *[A108/001398; SP4706]*

Adélie penguin turning eggs, November 1911. *[A108/001399; SP4707]*

A discussion between three Adélie penguins, November 1911. *[A108/001400; SP4708]*

A discussion between three Adélie penguins grows hotter, November 1911. *[A108/001401; SP4709]*

A discussion between three Adélie penguins becomes still hotter, November 1911. *[A108/001402; SP4710]*

A discussion between three Adélie penguins becomes a nose-pulling contest, November 1911. *[A108/001403; SP4711]*

A discussion between three Adélie penguins ends by one party getting a good licking, November 1911. *[A108/001404; SP4712]*

Penguin advertisement for Lyle's syrup, November 1911. *[A108/001406; SP4714]*

Penguin and chicks, January 9, 1911. *[A108/001407; SP4715]*

Penguin and chicks, January 9, 1911. *[A108/001408; SP4716]*

Penguin and chicks, January 9, 1911. *[A108/001409; SP4717]*

Penguin and chicks, January 9, 1911. *[A108/001410; SP4718]*

Penguin and chicks, January 9, 1911. *[A108/001411; SP4719]*

Penguin and chicks, January 9, 1911. *[A108/001412; SP4720]*

Penguin and chicks, January 9, 1911. *[A108/001413; SP4721]*

Penguin and chicks, January 9, 1911. *[A108/001414; SP4722]*

Penguin and chicks, January 9, 1911. *[A108/001415; SP4723]*

Penguin and chicks, January 9, 1911. *[A108/001416; SP4724]*

Penguin and chicks, January 9, 1911. *[A108/001417; SP4725]*

Penguin and chicks, January 9, 1911. *[A108/001418; SP4726]*

Penguin and chicks, January 9, 1911. *[A108/001419; SP4727]*

Penguin and chicks, January 9, 1911. *[A108/001420; SP4728]*

Reflections, penguinery. Cape Royds, January 9, 1911. *[A108/001422; SP4730]*

Pair of Adélie penguins, 1910–1912. *[A108/001479; SP4787]*

Group of Adélies on sea ice, 1910–1912. *[A108/001480; SP4788]*

Adélie penguin just jumped on to a floe, 1910–1912. *[A108/001481; SP4789]*

Adélie penguin leaping out of the water, 1910–1912. *[A108/001482; SP4790]*

Adélie penguin feeding young, 1910–1912. *[A108/001523; SP4831]*

Adélie penguin and young begging for food, 1910–1912. *[A108/001525; SP4833]*

Adélie penguins tobogganing, 1910–1912. *[A108/001526; SP4834]*

Emperor penguins on the heavy pancake ice, 1912. *[A108/001266; SP4574]*

An Emperor penguin, 1910–1912. *[A108/001484; SP4792]*

An Emperor penguin, 1910–1912. *[A108/001486; SP4794]*

A skua gull, January 6, 1911. *[A108/000828; SP4136]*

Skua gulls, male and female, January 6, 1911. *[A108/000829; SP4137]*

Skua gull's eggs in nest, January 6, 1911. *[A108/000830; SP4138]*

Skua and chick, a few days old, January 6, 1911. *[A108/000832; SP4140]*

Skua gull and chick, January 6, 1911. *[A108/000833; SP4141]*

Skua gull and chick, January 6, 1911. *[A108/000834; SP4142]*

Skua chick about one week old, January 6, 1911. *[A108/000835; SP4143]*

Skua gull bringing food to chick, January 6, 1911. *[A108/000836; SP4144]*

Gulls by hole in skua lake and Mt. Erebus, December 19, 1911. *[A108/001178; SP4486]*

Skua's nest and situation, January 1912. *[A108/001209; SP4517]*

Skua by nest and eggs, January 1912. *[A108/001211; SP4519]*

Skua by nest and eggs, January 1912. *[A108/001212; SP4520]*

Skua returning to eggs, January 1912. *[A108/001213; SP4521]*

Skua returning to eggs, January 1912. *[A108/001214; SP4522]*

Skua settling on eggs, January 1912. *[A108/001216; SP4524]*

Skua sitting, January 1912. *[A108/001217; SP4525]*

Skua sitting, January 1912. *[A108/001218; SP4526]*

Skuas bathing in lake, January 1912. *[A108/001219; SP4527]*

Skuas bathing in lake, January 1912. *[A108/001220; SP4528]*

Skua by nest and chick, January 1912. *[A108/001221; SP4529]*

Skua by nest and chick, January 1912. *[A108/001222; SP4530]*

Skua gull waiting to steal penguin eggs, November 1911. *[A108/001405; SP4713]*

Skuas picking a seal skin, 1910–1912. *[A108/001485; SP4793]*

Cape pigeon flying, December 1910. *[A108/001529; SP4837]*

Cape pigeon flying, December 1910. *[A108/001531; SP4839]*

Albatrosses foraging astern of *Terra Nova*, 1910–1912. *[A108/000791; SP4099]*

Albatrosses foraging astern of *Terra Nova*, 1910–1912. *[A108/000792; SP4100]*

Albatrosses in wake of *Terra Nova*, December 1910. *[A108/001532; SP4840]*

Albatross on the wing, 1910–1912. *[A108/001534; SP4842]*

Seals basking on new floe off Cape Evans, March 7, 1911. *[A108/000943; SP4251]*

Seals basking on new floe off Cape Evans, March 7, 1911. *[A108/000944; SP4252]*

Weddell seal. Cape Evans, March 15, 1911. *[A108/000962; SP4270]*

Weddell seal. Cape Evans, March 15, 1911. *[A108/000963; SP4271]*

Weddell seal. Cape Evans, March 15, 1911. *[A108/000964; SP4272]*

Weddell seal and newly born calf at Razorback, November 9, 1911. *[A108/001120; SP4428]*

Newly born Weddell seal calf at Razorback, November 9, 1911. *[A108/001121; SP4429]*

Weddell seal suckling calf, November 9, 1911. *[A108/001122; SP4430]*

Weddell seal suckling calf, November 9, 1911. *[A108/001123; SP4431]*

Weddell seal suckling calf, November 9, 1911. *[A108/001124; SP4432]*

Weddell seal and calf at Razorback, November 9, 1911. *[A108/001125; SP4433]*

Weddell seal and calf at Razorback, November 9, 1911. *[A108/001126; SP4434]*

Weddell seal and calf at Razorback, November 9, 1911. *[A108/001127; SP4435]*

Weddell seal and calf at Razorback, November 9, 1911. *[A108/001130; SP4438]*

Weddell seal and calf at Razorback, November 9, 1911. *[A108/001131; SP4439]*

Weddell seal and calf at Razorback, November 9, 1911. *[A108/001132; SP4440]*

Weddell seal and calf at Razorback, November 9, 1911. *[A108/001133; SP4441]*

Weddell seal and calf at Razorback, November 9, 1911. *[A108/001134; SP4442]*

Weddell seal enraged with calf at Razorback, November 9, 1911. *[A108/001135; SP4443]*

Tide crack and seal hole at Razorback, November 19, 1911. *[A108/001136; SP4444]*

Seals, Mt. Erebus, and Razorback (south), November 19, 1911. *[A108/001137; SP4445]*

Seal getting out of hole, November 19, 1911. *[A108/001139; SP4447]*

Seal with two young calves, alarmed, November 19, 1911. *[A108/001140; SP4448]*

Seal with two calves, November 19, 1911. *[A108/001141; SP4449]*

Seal with calf, November 19, 1911. *[A108/001143; SP4451]*

Seal with calf, November 19, 1911. *[A108/001144; SP4452]*

Seals at Razorback, November 19, 1911. *[A108/001146; SP4454]*

Seal with two calves, November 19, 1911. *[A108/001147; SP4455]*

Seals lying by Church Berg. Precipice effect, December 29, 1911. *[A108/001198; SP4506]*

Front of Turk's Head Glacier looking north with seal, January 1912. *[A108/001228; SP4536]*

Seal rising among ice floes, 1910–1912. *[A108/001471; SP4779]*

Seal rising among ice floes, 1910–1912. *[A108/001472; SP4780]*

Weddell seal. Cape Evans, 1910–1912. *[A108/001473; SP4781]*

Weddell seal. Cape Evans, 1910–1912. *[A108/001474; SP4782]*

Weddell seal. Cape Evans, 1910–1912. *[A108/001477; SP4785]*

Weddell seal. Cape Evans, 1910–1912. *[A108/001478; SP4786]*

A seal in brash ice, 1910–1912. *[A108/001492; SP4800]*

A seal in brash ice, 1910–1912. *[A108/001493; SP4801]*

A seal in brash ice, 1910–1912. *[A108/001495; SP4803]*

Seal and two calves, 1910–1912. *[A108/001527; SP4835]*

Weddell seal at Cape Evans, 1910–1912. *[A108/001528; SP4836]*

Seal and two calves, 1910–1912. *[A108/001530; SP4838]*

A sea leopard, May 28, 1911. *[A108/001013; SP4321]*

Forde and sea leopard, May 28, 1911. *[A108/001014; SP4322]*

Some of the ponies on *Terra Nova*, 1910–1912. *[A108/000787; SP4095]*

Interior of stable, March 28, 1911. *[A108/000975; SP4283]*

Evans and Crean with ponies on the ice, May 30, 1911. *[A108/001016; SP4324]*

Doctor Wilson and pony Nobby, October 1911. *[A108/001080; SP4388]*

Doctor Wilson and pony Nobby, October 1911. *[A108/001081; SP4389]*

Mr. Cherry-Garrard and pony Michael, October 1911. *[A108/001083; SP4391]*

P. O. Evans and pony Snatcher, October 1911. *[A108/001088; SP4396]*

Ponies picketed on the sea ice, January 1911. *[A108/001312; SP4620]*

Doctor Wilson, Lieutenant Bowers, Cherry-Garrard, and ponies on the sea ice, October 6, 1911. *[A108/001338; SP4646]*

Head of pony Victor, November 1911. *[A108/001357; SP4665]*

Heads of ponies in stable, 1910–1912. *[A108/001424; SP4732]*

Heads of ponies in stable, 1910–1912. *[A108/001426; SP4734]*

Husky Wolk, 1910–1912. *[A108/001430; SP4738]*

Husky Wolk, 1910–1912. *[A108/001432; SP4740]*

Husky Kasoi, 1910–1912. *[A108/001434; SP4742]*

Husky Kasoi, 1910–1912. *[A108/001435; SP4743]*

Husky Vaida, 1910–1912. *[A108/001437; SP4745]*

Husky Vaida, 1910–1912. *[A108/001441; SP4749]*

Husky Vaida, 1910–1912. *[A108/001442; SP4750]*

Husky Vaida, 1910–1912. *[A108/001443; SP4751]*

Husky Vaida, 1910–1912. *[A108/001444; SP4752]*

Husky Vaida, 1910–1912. *[A108/001445; SP4753]*

Husky Stareek, 1910–1912. *[A108/001448; SP4756]*

Husky Stareek, 1910–1912. *[A108/001449; SP4757]*

Husky Stareek, 1910–1912. *[A108/001450; SP4758]*

Husky Ostrenos, 1910–1912. *[A108/001451; SP4759]*

Husky Ostrenos, 1910–1912. *[A108/001452; SP4760]*

Husky Krisravitsa, 1910–1912. *[A108/001457; SP4765]*

Husky Krisravitsa, 1910–1912. *[A108/001459; SP4767]*

Husky Krisravitsa, 1910–1912. *[A108/001460; SP4768]*

Husky Krisravitsa, 1910–1912. *[A108/001461; SP4769]*

Husky Krisravitsa, 1910–1912. *[A108/001462; SP4770]*

Husky Krisravitsa, 1910–1912. *[A108/001463; SP4771]*

Husky Osman, 1910–1912. *[A108/001465; SP4773]*

Husky Osman, 1910–1912. *[A108/001466; SP4774]*

Husky Osman, 1910–1912. *[A108/001468; SP4776]*

Killer whale rising in hole in ice, 1912. *[A108/001263; SP4571]*

A rorqual off Glacier Tongue, 1910–1912. *[A108/001489; SP4797]*

A whale diving under the ice, 1910–1912. *[A108/001490; SP4798]*

A shark off New Zealand, 1910–1912. *[A108/001548; SP4856]*

The squid found by Ponting and captured by him and Lashly at Cape Royds, February 16, 1911. *[A108/000919; SP4227]*

Landscapes

Sunset effect, Antarctic Circle, December 8, 1910. *[A108/000745; SP4053]*

Detail of the pack, December 11, 1910. *[A108/000756; SP4064]*

Telephoto of tilted barrier berg, December 18, 1910. *[A108/000764; SP4072]*

The berg that resembled an island, December 19, 1910. *[A108/000766; SP4074]*

Telephoto. Berg in pack. Debenham and Taylor on the ice, December 20, 1910. *[A108/000768; SP4076]*

Light effect on pack, December 22, 1910. *[A108/000771; SP4079]*

Detail of floe and penguins, December 24, 1910. *[A108/000774; SP4082]*

A lead opening in the pack, December 28, 1910. *[A108/000777; SP4085]*

Pack breaking up, December 28, 1910. *[A108/000779; SP4087]*

Detail of pack with penguins, December 28, 1910. *[A108/000780; SP4088]*

Typical piece of floating ice, January 1, 1911. *[A108/000799; SP4107]*

Typical piece of floating ice, January 1, 1911. *[A108/000800; SP4108]*

Ross Sea. Open water and clouds. Noon, January 2, 1911. *[A108/000801; SP4109]*

Ross Sea. Open water and clouds. Noon, January 2, 1911. *[A108/000802; SP4110]*

Mt. Terror about noon, January 3, 1911. *[A108/000807; SP4115]*

Ice blink over the Barrier, January 3, 1911. *[A108/000808; SP4116]*

View of the Barrier at 1:45 p.m., January 3, 1911. *[A108/000809; SP4117]*

The Barrier and Mt. Terror, 2:00 p.m., January 3, 1911. *[A108/000810; SP4118]*

Cape Crozier. Precipes, January 3, 1911. *[A108/000813; SP4121]*

Killer whale off the penguin rookery, January 3, 1911. *[A108/000815; SP4123]*

Mt. Terror at 6:00 p.m., January 3, 1911. *[A108/000816; SP4124]*

Mt. Terror at 6.30 p.m., January 3, 1911. *[A108/000817; SP4125]*

Mt. Erebus at 11:00 p.m., January 3, 1911. *[A108/000819; SP4127]*

Mt. Bird at 11:00 p.m., January 3, 1911. *[A108/000821; SP4129]*

Mt. Erebus at 1:15 a.m., January 4, 1911. *[A108/000822; SP4130]*

Pool below cascade, January 7, 1911. *[A108/000843; SP4151]*

The cavern in the iceberg. *Terra Nova* in the distance, January 8, 1911. *[A108/000850; SP4158]*

Detail of sea ice breaking up, January 9, 1911. *[A108/000853; SP4161]*

Cumulus cloud on Barne Glacier, January 13, 1911. *[A108/000860; SP4168]*

Mt. Erebus and stranded berg. Made just when ship struck, January 20, 1911. *[A108/000873; SP4181]*

Stranded berg and boat coming off, January 20, 1911. *[A108/000876; SP4184]*

Mt. Erebus and whaling boat in foreground, January 20, 1911. *[A108/000877; SP4185]*

Ice showing morainic cones on Green Lake. Cape Royds, February 15, 1911. *[A108/000912; SP4220]*

Sastrugi on Barne Glacier, February 21, 1911. *[A108/000928; SP4236]*

Sastrugi on Barne Glacier, February 21, 1911. *[A108/000929; SP4237]*

Wave at West Beach, February 28, 1911. *[A108/000931; SP4239]*

Wave breaking at West Beach, February 28, 1911. *[A108/000934; SP4242]*

Wave breaking at West Beach, February 28, 1911. *[A108/000935; SP4243]*

Wave breaking at West Beach, February 28, 1911. *[A108/000936; SP4244]*

Wave breaking at West Beach, February 28, 1911. *[A108/000937; SP4245]*

Wave breaking at West Beach, February 28, 1911. *[A108/000938; SP4246]*

Cloud effect on Mt. Erebus at noon, March 7, 1911. *[A108/000939; SP4247]*

Mt. Erebus and dome cloud from West Beach, 2:30 p.m., icicled glacier in foreground, March 7, 1911. *[A108/000940; SP4248]*

Weathered Kenyte boulder near house, March 8, 1911. *[A108/000948; SP4256]*

Weathered Kenyte boulder near house. "The Antarcticossauras," March 8, 1911. *[A108/000949; SP4257]*

Weathered ice after blizzard at Cape Evans, looking to Castle Rock, March 8, 1911. *[A108/000950; SP4258]*

Spray ridges of ice, Cape Evans. Inaccessible Island in the distance, March 8, 1911. *[A108/000951; SP4259]*

Weathered ice furrows after a blizzard at Cape Evans and crevasse, looking south toward Turks Head, March 8, 1911. *[A108/000953; SP4261]*

Morainic cones, Mt. Erebus in background. Day on top, March 9, 1911. *[A108/000954; SP4262]*

"Frost smoke" on North Bay, March 13, 1911. *[A108/000958; SP4266]*

Clouds on Mt. Erebus, 8:45 a.m., March 26, 1911. *[A108/000973; SP4281]*

The Castle Berg with dog sledge, September 17, 1911. *[A108/001054; SP4362]*

Huge ice bastions of the Castle Berg (Clissold at base), September 17, 1911. *[A108/001055; SP4363]*

A great bastion of ice, September 17, 1911. *[A108/001057; SP4365]*

Under the lee of the Castle Berg, September 17, 1911. *[A108/001058; SP4366]*

The point of the Barne Glacier (where it turns round to the Bay before Cape Barne), September 18, 1911. *[A108/001060; SP4368]*

The Matterhorn Berg, profile (Clissold on summit), October 8, 1911. *[A108/001072; SP4380]*

Summit of Mt. Erebus, October 1911. *[A108/001107; SP4415]*

Hut Point and Vince Cross looking south, November 4, 1911. *[A108/001112; SP4420]*

A view of Hut Point, November 4, 1911. *[A108/001114; SP4422]*

Castle Rock, November 5, 1911. *[A108/001118; SP4426]*

Midnight Sun effect on Mt. Discovery taken from one mile south of Razorback at 11:00 p.m., November 5, 1911. *[A108/001119; SP4427]*

The pillar at Cape Barne, November 29, 1911. *[A108/001149; SP4457]*

Pinnacle of Church Berg and icicles with Anton, December 29, 1911. *[A108/001201; SP4510]*

Telephoto, Mt. Discovery, 1912. *[A108/001225; SP4533]*

Ice breaking up off Cape Evans, January 30, 1912. *[A108/001234; SP4542]*

Cloud effect over Barne Glacier, 1912. *[A108/001256; SP4564]*

Cloud effect over Barne Glacier, 1912. *[A108/001257; SP4565]*

Heavy pancake ice (several feet thick in layers) in which ship was held whilst trying to rescue the Northern Party, 1912. *[A108/001264; SP4572]*

Heavy pancake ice with floes, 1912. *[A108/001267; SP4575]*

Frost smoke off Glacier Tongue, 1912. *[A108/001273; SP4581]*

Wake of *Terra Nova* in new pancake ice, 1912. *[A108/001277; SP4585]*

Iceberg passed on voyage home, 1912. *[A108/001279; SP4587]*

Iceberg passed on voyage home, 1912. *[A108/001280; SP4588]*

Sledger at the foot of glacier and Mt. Erebus, 1912. *[A108/001285; SP4593]*

Christmas Eve in the pack, December, 1912. *[A108/001301; SP4609]*

Mt. Erebus at midnight from *Terra Nova* off Cape Bird, January 3, 1911. *[A108/001304; SP4612]*

Cloud effect. Ross Sea, January 2, 1911. *[A108/001305; SP4613]*

Mt. Erebus at midnight from the *Terra Nova* off Cape Bird, January 3, 1911. *[A108/001306; SP4614]*

The ice foot looking to Cape Royds from *Terra Nova*, January 1911. *[A108/001308; SP4616]*

Looking to Cape Barne from Cape Evans: mirage effect, March 3, 1911. *[A108/001317; SP4625]*

Iceberg off Cape Evans, March 1911. *[A108/001319; SP4627]*

Looking to Cape Barne from Cape Evans: mirage effect, March 3, 1911. *[A108/001320; SP4628]*

Cloud effect, North Bay and Barne Glacier, March 26, 1911. *[A108/001322; SP4630]*

Cloud effect in the Sound, March 26, 1911. *[A108/001324; SP4632]*

First appearance of the Sun over Barne Glacier, August 26, 1911. *[A108/001331; SP4639]*

Cloud effect on ice. Cape Royds, November 27, 1911. *[A108/001362; SP4670]*

Cloud effect on ice. Cape Royds, November 1911. *[A108/001363; SP4671]*

Frost smoke off Glacier Tongue, 1910–1912. *[A108/001494; SP4802]*

Frost smoke off Glacier Tongue, 1910–1912. *[A108/001497; SP4805]*

Sunset. Antarctic Ocean with gull, 1910–1912. *[A108/001515; SP4823]*